Presented as a gift from Oorah TorahMates

We hope you enjoy this book.

1.877.TORAH-123 • www.torahmates.org

ArtScroll Series®

Rabbi Nosson Scherman / Rabbi Meir Zlotowitz

General Editors

BASED ON A SERIES OF LECTURES BY
RABBI YITZCHAK BERKOWITZ
BY RABBI YEHUDA HEIMOWITZ
IN COLLABORATION WITH RABBI SHAI MARKOWITZ

OVERVIEW BY
RABBI NOSSON SCHERMAN

Published by
Mesorah Publications, ltd

שש מצות תמידיות

the 6 CONSTANT MITZVOS

THE TORAH'S FRAMEWORK
FOR DEVELOPING
A MEANINGFUL RELATIONSHIP
WITH HASHEM — CONSTANTLY

FIRST EDITION
First Impression … September 2009
Second Impression … November 2010
SECOND EDITION
Sixth Impressions … June 2011 — March 2021
Seventh Impression … November 2022

Published and Distributed by
MESORAH PUBLICATIONS, LTD.
313 Regina Avenue / Rahway, N.J. 07065

Distributed in Europe by
LEHMANNS
Unit E, Viking Industrial Park
Rolling Mill Road
Jarrow, Tyne & Wear NE32 3DP
England

Distributed in Australia & New Zealand by
GOLDS WORLD OF JUDAICA
3-13 William Street
Balaclava, Melbourne 3183
Victoria Australia

Distributed in Israel by
SIFRIATI / A. GITLER — BOOKS
POB 2351
Bnei Brak 51122

Distributed in South Africa by
KOLLEL BOOKSHOP
Northfield Centre, 17 Northfield Avenue
Glenhazel 2192, Johannesburg, South Africa

ARTSCROLL® SERIES
THE SIX CONSTANT MITZVOS
© Copyright 2009, by MESORAH PUBLICATIONS, Ltd.
313 Regina Avenue / Rahway, N.J. 07065 / (718) 921-9000 / www.artscroll.com

ISBN 10: 1-4226-0926-X / ISBN 13: 978-1-4226-0926-2
ITEM CODE: SIXH

Typography by CompuScribe at ArtScroll Studios, Ltd.
Printed in United States of America
Bound by Sefercraft, Quality Bookbinders, Ltd., Rahway, NJ

בס"ד

שמואל קמנצקי
Rabbi S. Kamenetsky

2018 Upland Way
Philadelphia, Pa 19131

Home: 215-473-2798
Study: 215-473-1212

ז' כסלו, תש"ע

כתב הרמב"ם בפירוש המשניות (ברכות פ"ט סוף משנה ה'), וז"ל: דרכי
תמיד בכל מקום שיש איזה רמז בעניני אמונה אבאר, כי חשוב אצלי
להסביר יסוד מהיסודות יותר מכל דבר אחר שאני מלמד. מצות האמונה
היא הראשונה והשרשית מבן שש המצות תמידיות, המצות שחיובן תמידי
ולא יפסקו מעל האדם אפילו רגע אחד כל ימיו

החפץ חיים בספרו משנה ברורה בתחילת הביאור הלכה ביאר שכדי לקיים
את ההלכה הראשונה בשו"ע "שויתי ה' לנגדי תמיד, צריך האדם לקיים את
השש מצות והאריך בביאור כל השש מצות תמידיות.

וכמו בכל מצוה ומצוה - אי אפשר לקיימה אלא אם לומדים אותה
ומעמיקים בה היטב, ללמוד את דיניה ופרטיה וכל דקדוקיה, כך בשש
מצות אלו צריך כל אדם ללמוד אותם, ללמוד את דרך קיומם, וגם ללמוד
ולהתעורר מדברי מוסר המחזקים את הלב - לתת את לבו כדי לקיימם
בהידור

והנה עתה בא לפני הרב שי מרקוביץ שליט"א, עם קסטות של שיעורים
מהרה"ג ר' יצחק שליט"א על השש מצות תמידיות, ובידו גם ספר שכתב
כדי לחזק לבני הישיבות בלימוד השש מצות התמידיות ובפרט במצות
אמונה. הספר מבוסס על השיעורים של הרה"ג ר' יצחק ברקוביץ מגדולי
התורה ויר"ש, והוא ראש כולל ומשפיע בירושלים, שמו הולך לפניו וכבר
אתמחי לגברא רבה, וכדאי הוא לסמוך עליו

ועל ידי לימוד זה יתעורר אצל מורים ומורות תלמידים ותלמידות שיבינו
הענין בתוקפו ולאמיתו ובודאי עי"ז יצליחו להשריש בלבם אמונת ה'
אמיתית ויצליחו בלמודם מעלה מעלה.

והנני בברכה להרב שי מרקוביץ שליט"א שיצליח בכל מעשה ידיו ויזכה
להמנות ממזכי הרבים ובזכות הלימוד הקדוש הזה, יעלו התלמידים מחיל
אל חיל אמן

כ"ג אייר תשס"ט

יתיב הוינא ואתה לקדמנא הרב הנעלה והמצוין ר' יהודה הייומוביץ שליט"א ועמו
צרור כתבים בעניינים העומדים ברומו של עולם ובחובתו של כל אחד ואחד, שש
מצוות התמידיות המוזכרים בדברי רבנו בעל החינוך זת"ע. הנה המחבר היקר
למד בישיבתנו הק' לפני נישואיו ומאז לא מש מתוך האהל ועלה שם במעלות
התורה. יראת שמים היא אוצרו הטוב ואהוב על חבריו ורבותיו במדות טובות שמנו
חכמים. עתה כאשר נתן עינו ולבו לעיין בענין הנ"ל ולהעלות מסקנתיו על הגליון
ולהפיץ מעיינותיו לתועלת הרבים, אמרתי לברכו שחפץ ה' יצליח בידו ויתגלגל
זכות על ידי זכאי כמוהו לעורר את הרבים ולחזקם לקיום הדברים כראוי. יהי רצון
שיזכה לשבת על התורה ועל העבודה ללמוד וללמד לשמר ולעשות ולקיים את כל
דברי התוה"ק ולהאיר עיני הרבים במאור התורה.

הכו"ח בכבוד ויקר

הרב נתן צבי פינקל
ראש הישיבה

Rabbi Yitzchak Berkovits
Sanhedria HaMurchevet 113/27
Jerusalem, Israel 97707
02-5813847

יצחק שמואל הלוי ברקוביץ
ראש רשת הכוללים לינת הצדק
סנהדרי"ה המורחבת 113/27
ירושלם ת"ו

בס"ד ירושלם ת"ו י"ג אנ_רא תשס"ט

This generation has *baruch HaShem* witnessed growth of the Torah world in proportions unprecedented in hundreds of years. We have also been *zocheh* to a level of *dikduk b'mitzvos* previously reserved for unique individuals famous for their *yir'as chet*. Yet, a true fulfillment of the *mitzvos* of *emunah* -the cornerstone of Judaism- and a sophisticated understanding of these commandments has yet to assume its proper place among the masses of *b'nei Torah*.

This work, based on classes given to a group of *b'nei aliyah* at Aish HaTorah years ago, is a serious attempt at filling that void. I am indebted to my dear friend Rabbi Shai Markowitz whom I had the privilege of teaching at The Jerusalem Kollel for making this project happen. His very positive experiences in teaching the sheish mizvos to *b'nei Yeshivah* served as an inspiration for his endless dedication to putting the ideas to print. I am appreciative of the countless hours invested by the writer Rabbi Yehuda Heimowitz and the priority given this project by Artscroll.

May *HaShem* open the hearts of so many Jews dedicated to His Torah, and bless us with true *emunah, ahavas Hashem* and *Yir'as Shamayim*.

Appreciatively,

Rabbi Avraham Schorr

1860 52nd Street
Brooklyn NY 11204
718 232-6145

אברהם הלוי שארר
רב דקהל תפארת יעקב
1212 East Fifteenth Street
Brooklyn, NY 11230

בס״ד

כבוד ידידי הרה״ג מוהר״ר כו׳

שמחתי אל הדברים שנכתבו בשבח התורשת ואחז ולראה
הם מאמת תמימיות, אשר ע״י רמזו בספרן שהעיר
הדבר ע״פ אלאית מפורים, והדברים שצנרו בינור טוב,
והנה ועוסרים של אדני בכתי הראשונים אשר מאתם
ינק אמרית, ופל הדברית הם נעירים מאור בדורו
אשר האמונה ושאמית התשצת באון שהי האלו
דברן כבנראו וצושה רצון הך תמ״ל. ולכן אאוקא
לאחל בר״ש, וירוה הדברים מקובדים בי מראל
מאות תמיד, וליראה איתה של דורין ולהרר אל
ינא התויית.

פרים כו מ שושמן כלב
ידיד הלוי שארר

TABLE OF CONTENTS

CONSTANT MITZVAH 1:
אֱמוּנָה בַּה'
Faith in Hashem

לזכר נשמת

ז"ל Mr. Harry Markowitz — ר' נח צבי בן ר' דוב ז"ל

CONSTANT MITZVAH 2:
לֹא יִהְיֶה
Not to Believe in Other Gods

CONSTANT MITZVAH 3:

יִחוּד ה׳
Hashem's Oneness

לזכר נשמות

ר׳ משה בן ר׳ אברהם שלום הכהן ז״ל
ר׳ צבי הירש בן ר׳ שרגא פייוויל ז״ל
ר׳ שמואל משה בן ר׳ שמחה ז״ל

CONSTANT MITZVAH 4:

אַהֲבַת ה׳
Loving Hashem

לזכר נשמות

ישראל יהודה ב״ר יוסף דוב ז״ל רעבענווארצעל
ורעיתו **יעקפקע יהודית בת ר׳ אברהם ע״ה**
שמואל צבי ב״ר משה ז״ל הרמן
ורעיתו **שיינדל יפה בת ר׳ יצחק ע״ה**

CONSTANT MITZVAH 5:

יִרְאַת ה׳
Fearing Hashem

Dedicated on the occasion of the engagement
of our children **Shiffie Goldenberg** to **Yoni Merzel**

CONSTANT MITZVAH 6:

שֶׁלֹּא לָתוּר אַחַר מַחֲשֶׁבֶת הַלֵּב וּרְאִיַּת הָעֵינַיִם
Do Not Stray After Your Heart and Eyes

A Note to the Reader:

For the convenience of readers who would like to read this work as a daily program, we have noted appropriate divisions in the margins.

Publisher's Preface

It is our great privilege to present the *Six Constant Mitzvos* to the Jewish public. The more we discussed and became familiar with the subject and the skill with which it is presented, the more we became convinced that it is an important — even an essential — service to the public. The classic *Sefer HaChinuch* urges people to have these commandments in mind constantly, and the Chofetz Chaim not only agreed, but considered it so important that he summarized these commandments at relative length at the very beginning of *Beur Halachah*.

This volume demonstrates skillfully, incisively, and literately that these commandments refine and elevate a Jew and provide a framework for a lifetime of spiritual growth and service. It is a book not only enjoyable to read, but it leaves the reader with food for thought and motivation to act on its messages.

This work is based on a series of lectures by Rabbi Yitzchak Berkowitz, an eminent *posek*, *rosh kollel*, thinker, and Rav in Jerusalem. We are grateful to him for permitting his teachings to be presented to the broad Torah public.

The book was written primarily by Rabbi Yehuda Heimowitz, an outstanding scholar and writer in Jerusalem. He is familiar to ArtScroll readers from his work on such best-selling new classics as *Wisdom in the Hebrew Months* and Rabbi Yissocher Frand's work on

the weekly *parashah*. We look forward to many years of his partici-
pation in our work and are grateful for the opportunity to make his
talent available to the public.

The idea for this book was conceived by Rabbi Shai Markowitz,
who was the first to recognize the enormous potential of this
work, and who collaborated with Rabbi Heimowitz in producing
it. Rabbi Markowitz is man of rare sensitivity and dedication to
the strengthening of Torah life and to bringing its message to the
broader community.

We are confident that this work will do an enormous amount of
good and that leaders, teachers, and readers will share in our grati-
tude to those who collaborated to bring the lectures to the printed
page.

Rabbi Meir Zlotowitz / Rabbi Nosson Scherman

Elul 5769 / September 2009

Acknowledgments

It is a privilege and an honor for me to present to the Jewish public a revised edition of *The Six Constant Mitzvos*. The incredible feedback to the first edition and the different initiatives I have run for the public have encouraged and inspired me to work on and complete this revised edition.

It is obvious that a work of this scope — taking deep, philosophical Torah thoughts and transforming them into clear and enjoyable prose — could not have been successful without the collaborative efforts of many talented and dedicated people. I could not possibly thank all those people, but I would like to mention several individuals who were particularly instrumental in making this revised edition appear.

I thank Rav Shmuel Kamenetsky, *shlit"a*, Philadelphia Rosh Yeshivah, and Rav Mattisyahu Salomon, *shlit"a*, Mashgiach of Beis Medrash Govoha, Lakewood, who took time from their ever-busy schedules to discuss with me the importance of the *limud* of the Six Constant Mitzvos and to offer various suggestions of how to spread this *limud* throughout Klal Yisrael.

I am grateful to the *Ribbono shel Olam* for giving me the incredible privilege to build a very special relationship with Rav Avrohom Schorr, *shlit"a*, Rav of Khal Tiferes Yaakov; without his initial and continued daily encouragement, this *sefer* would not have been published.

From beginning to end I was guided by the ArtScroll family, led by Rabbi Meir Zlotowitz and Rabbi Nosson Scherman. I greatly appreciate the wisdom and care that they invested in this *sefer*.

I would also like to specifically thank Mrs. Mindy Stern for her proofreading and editing of this revised edition.

Rabbi Yitzchak Berkowitz, *shlit"a*, Rosh Kollel of The Jerusalem Kollel, originally gave these *shiurim* through the encouragement of Rav Noach Weinberg, *zt'l*, and it was Rav Noach's dream to spread this *limud* throughout the world. I am humbled, yet honored, to have been able to be a part of bringing his life dream to fruition. A special thank you to Rav Hillel Weinberg, *shlit"a*, and Rabbi Yitzchok (Eric) Coopersmith.

A tremendous *yasher koach* to Rabbi Abi Goldenberg and his immediate and extended family for all the sacrifice and encouragement they continue to give us in our עֲבוֹדַת הַקֹּדֶשׁ.

I owe a special *hakoras hatov* to Aryeh Weiss, who has been a source of support, encouragement, and assistance in more ways than I can mention.

Just a few short months ago, I was privileged to be introduced to Shai Stern, someone whose enthusiasm and excitement for Yiddishkiet and specifically The Six Constant Mitzvos inspires me — constantly. Thank you.

I am honored and privileged to be able to work together with David and Deena Zaitzchek. Their advice, encouragement, and real-life example continue to inspire me in all that I do.

My greatest debt of appreciation and my most special thanks are due to my *aishes chayil*, Rivka Tova — "שֶׁלִּי וְשֶׁלָּכֶם שֶׁלָּהּ הוּא" (*Kesubos* 63a). She has been my rock and strength in all our endeavors. Besides taking care of our *mishpachah* and everything else, her continued encouragement has been the backbone of this whole project. As the mothers of Klal Yisrael say in their *tefillos* each Friday night by candle-lighting: וְזַכֵּנוּ לְגַדֵּל בָּנִים וּבְנֵי בָנִים חֲכָמִים וּנְבוֹנִים

אוֹהֲבֵי ה׳ יִרְאֵי אֱלֹקִים אַנְשֵׁי אֱמֶת זֶרַע קֹדֶשׁ בַּהּ׳ דְּבֵקִים וּמְאִירִים אֶת הָעוֹלָם בְּתוֹרָה וּבְמַעֲשִׂים טוֹבִים וּבְכָל מְלֶאכֶת עֲבוֹדַת הַבּוֹרֵא. May the *Ribbono shel Olam* grant us continued *nachas* from our wonderful children.

Finally, I thank Hashem for enabling me to transmit the values of the Six Constant Mitzvos to His people.

It is my heartfelt *tefillah* that this *sefer* succeeds in teaching Klal Yisrael the Torah's framework for living with *emunah* and its tools to develop a meaningful relationship with Hashem, and makes them feel and appreciate His constant presence in their lives.

Rabbi Shai Markowitz

Kislev, 5771

An Overview/
Mitzvos Make the Man

רַבִּי חֲנַנְיָא בֶּן עֲקַשְׁיָא אוֹמֵר: רָצָה הַקָּדוֹשׁ בָּרוּךְ
הוּא לְזַכּוֹת אֶת יִשְׂרָאֵל, לְפִיכָךְ הִרְבָּה לָהֶם תּוֹרָה
וּמִצְוֹת, שֶׁנֶּאֱמַר: ה' חָפֵץ לְמַעַן צִדְקוֹ יַגְדִּיל תּוֹרָה
וְיַאְדִּיר.

*Rabbi Chananya ben Akashya says: The
Holy One, Blessed is He, wanted to con-
fer merit upon Israel, therefore He gave
them an abundance of Torah and mitzvos, as [the verse] says (Yeshayah 42:21):
"Hashem desired for the sake of [Israel's]
righteousness that the Torah be make great
and glorious" (Makkos 23b).*

IN EXPOUNDING UPON THE ABOVE MISHNAH, THE
Talmud (ibid.) states that God gave 613 mitzvos
to the Jewish people, 248 positive and 365 negative
commandments. The Talmud goes on to say that
several of the prophets — King David, Yeshayah,
Michah, and Chavakkuk — recognized that there had
to be a simpler course, one within easier reach of the
masses of Jews, so they devised a "distilled" course
of service, as it were, in which they respectively
provided short lists of the essential components of
Divine service.*

*Several of
the prophets
recognized that
there had to be a
simpler course,
one within
easier reach of
the masses of
Jews.*

This, of course, does not mean that these prophets annulled even one of the God-given 613 commandments of the Torah. No one has the power to
do that. Nor does it mean that they designated some

---

* The Overview is based primarily on Maharal (Chiddushei Aggados and Tiferes Yisrael;
see also Aruch LaNer).

commandments as more important than others. As Rambam sets forth in the eighth and ninth Principles of Faith:

> I believe with complete faith that the entire Torah now in our hands is the same one that was given to Moshe, our teacher, peace be upon him.
>
> I believe with complete faith that this Torah will not be exchanged nor will there be another Torah from the Creator, blessed is His Name.

Let us seek to understand how the Torah's commandments shape the Jewish people and what the prophets intended when they composed short lists of essential commandments.

I. The Goal Is Closeness

Functions of the Mitzvos

IT IS THE MISSION AND THE HIGHEST GOAL OF EVERY Jew to achieve closeness to God. To enable us to do so the Torah gives us the commandments. As the designations "positive" and "negative" imply, these two classes of mitzvos have two different functions.

The positive commandments enable us to build a "spiritual superstructure" of good deeds.

The positive commandments enable us to build a "spiritual superstructure" of good deeds that enables us to grow and to attain the goal of subjugating the body to the soul, and to ascend the spiritual heights for which God created us. The negative commandments insulate us from deeds that break the rungs of the ladder leading to the achievement of the goal. For example, the commandment to eat matzah on Pesach achieves a spiritual purpose;

The negative commandments insulate us from deeds that break the rungs of the ladder.

the eating of *chametz* defeats that purpose. In a sense, the corpus of positive commandments is like a spiritual factory that will fashion the Jew into an entity worthy of uniting with God, while the negative commandments are the fences and alarms that prevent destructive forces from interfering with the sacred task.

The early Chassidic masters illustrated this concept with a metaphor. Every performance of a mitzvah is like a brick in the heavenly Holy Temple that, when completed, will descend to earth with the coming of the Messiah, but every sin causes the structure to collapse, so that the Jewish people must begin anew.

It is axiomatic that every one of the 613 commandments has its own unique spiritual power. Within each deed, there are varying degrees of perfection, depending on the degree of sincerity, knowledge, and dedication with which the individual Jew performed it. Therefore, ten people can perform the same commandment, but there will be ten different outcomes. Moshe, our teacher, wore *tefillin*, and an unlearned laborer, looking at the clock and anxious to get to work, wears *tefillin*. Both performed the identical act, but the quality of the two mitzvah-performances is hardly the same. Only God can know and measure the infinite gradations of worth in all we do and how well we do it.

Every performance of a mitzvah is like a brick in the heavenly Holy Temple, but every sin causes the structure to collapse.

Both performed the identical act, but the quality of the two mitzvah-performances is hardly the same.

How to Perform Them All

NEVERTHELESS, ONE THING IS CLEAR: FOR A human being to climb to his own Divinely ordained pinnacle of achievement, he must perform all 613 commandments. It would seem, however, that this is not possible. There are commandments involving the Temple service that can be performed only when there is a *Beis HaMikdash*; there are agricultural laws that apply only in the Holy Land; there are commandments that can be performed only by Kohanim or by people with the means to make loans or give charity. Some commandments can be performed only by repentant sinners, such as the commandment to return a stolen article or to make amends to those they have harmed. Surely we are not expected to steal or hurt a fellow human being so that we can make restitution or ask forgiveness. Clearly, therefore, no individual can perform all the commandments, especially during the exile.

Clearly, therefore, no individual can perform all the commandments, especially during the exile.

To remedy this apparent impossibility, the Sages have taught that one who studies the laws of a commandment that he cannot perform physically is considered as if he had actually performed the commandment. There is another element in the performance of commandments. To explain the greater quality of prayer with a *minyan*, as opposed to praying privately, *Kuzari* writes that few people can concentrate with the proper intent on the entire *Shemoneh Esrei*. But when there is a *minyan* that unites ten people in the joint performance of the *tefillah*, each one's devotion is credited to the group as a whole.

When there is a minyan that unites ten people in the joint performance of the tefillah, each one's devotion is credited to the group as a whole.

The same would apply to the nation as a whole. When the Jewish nation is united in its service of God, each individual doing what he can and what he must — Kohanim, farmers, the wealthy, the struggling worker, men, and women — they are no longer individual Jews; they are *Klal Yisrael*, and the sum is greater than the total of its parts, just as the prayer of a *minyan* is more powerful than that of ten Jews praying separately.

They are Klal Yisrael, and the sum is greater than the total of its parts.

In introducing the recitation of *Pirkei Avos* on the summer Shabbasos, we quote the Mishnah (*Sanhedrin* 90a): *All Israel has a share in the World to Come, as it is said: "And Your people are all righteous; they shall inherit the land forever, they are the branch of My planting, My handiwork, in which to take pride* (Yeshayah 60:21). Many commentators note homiletically that the prophet speaks of "all Israel" having a share in the World to Come, implying that when we serve God as a nation, and not only as private citizens, the entire nation is elevated.

In the words of Rabbi Samson Raphael Hirsch: "The term Israel refers to any individual who has not utterly divorced himself from Israel's lofty spiritual and ethical destiny. His portion in the World to Come will vary according to his merit, but as long as he remains part of Israel, he will never lose it entirely."

II. In the Divine Image

THE TORAH DESCRIBES ADAM AS HAVING BEEN created in the "image of God." Obviously it cannot be that God has physical organs, since it is a principle of our belief that God has no physical characteristics. What, then, was man's Divine image?

Maharal (*Derech Chaim* to *Pirkei Avos* 3:14) explains that just as God is the complete Master of the spiritual world and He has no parallel among even the loftiest angels and other spiritual beings, so too, man has uncontested superiority on earth. When animals walk, they look down, symbolizing that they are subservient, but man walks erect because he is their master. As God told Adam and Eve when He created them: *... fill the earth and subdue it; and rule over the fish of the sea, the bird of the sky, and every living thing that moves on the earth* (Bereishis 1:28). Only man stands erect, because in the earthly realm, he is master. God created him to be the king of Creation, just as God is the King of everything. It is in this sense that man was created in the "image of God."

True, the Torah speaks of God's "outstretched arm" and the prophet says that he saw *upon the likeness of [God's] throne there was a likeness like the appearance of a man upon it* (Yechezkel 1:26), and countless other verses that imply strongly that God has physicality. This is not the case, however. In order to give earthly man a concept of God's powers and deeds, Scripture describes them in the borrowed terms of human anatomy, which is the sort of depiction we can associate with.

In the terminology of Maharal and the Kabbalists, such descriptions are in the nature of a לְבוּשׁ, *garment*. When we see someone covered by clothing, we know that clothes are not the person, but the clothing helps us to visualize that there are arms and legs under the garments, and there are a mouth, eyes, ears, and a nose under the covering. We can visualize the height, weight, and build of the person, though we cannot see him.

So too, the borrowed terminology that ascribes organs to God. To visualize His power, we think of a Man of War's outstretched arm. To feel the awe of judgment, we imagine God presiding over the Heavenly Court, with us begging for mercy as we account for our horrendous sins and are embarrassed to show only puny good deeds in our defense.

Maharal cites another aspect of man's similarity to God, as it were. Godliness has a spiritual glow. The Sages describe the beauty of the World to Come as the righteous will sit and derive pleasure from זִיו הַשְּׁכִינָה, *the glow of the Divine Presence* (*Berachos* 17a). If man attains the goal God set for him, he, too, has a spiritual glow. Even ordinary Jews find themselves transfixed by the presence of holy Jews who have succeeded in perfecting themselves. No one in centuries has equaled the visage of Moshe, whose countenance shone with such a heavenly glow that his contemporaries could not bear to look at him, but first-person accounts down the centuries, even in our time, bear testimony that when the soul transcends the flesh, the transformation is visible on the face of such people.

If man attains the goal God set for him, he, too, has a spiritual glow.

This, too, is an aspect of man's likeness to God. Animals don't have it. Even angels don't have it, because angels — although infinitely greater than mortal man — are unchanging. God creates them for their role in His service, and they remain static, always performing their mission. Only man can grow and fashion himself into the image of God.

This, too, is an aspect of man's likeness to God. Only man can grow and fashion himself into the image of God.

Without
Limit

That growth should be constant. Man is never free of the obligation to grow, nor does he ever reach a stage when he can no longer grow. Rabbi Yitzchak Hutner cited the Midrash on the verse that states that when God completed the six days of Creation: וַיַּרְא אֱלֹקִים אֶת כָּל אֲשֶׁר עָשָׂה וְהִנֵּה טוֹב מְאֹד, *And God saw all that He had made, and behold it was very good* (*Bereishis* 1:31). Throughout the chapter of Creation, whenever God completed a part of the universe, there is the refrain *And God saw that it was good*. Only at the end of the sixth day does the Torah say it was *very* good. What was it now that earned the superlative adjective?

The Midrash says that the word מְאֹד, *very*, refers to אָדָם, *man*. Everything was good — but man was *very* good. In the simple sense, one assumes that the implication is because the Hebrew words for "very" and "man" — מְאֹד and אָדָם — are comprised of the same letters. Rabbi Hutner explained that the teaching of the Sages is much deeper than a simple play on words. The word "very" has no specific definition. How much is "very"? A yard? A furlong? A mile? It is all of these and more. The word "very" has no defined limit. Man's capacity, too, has no limit. He can grow and grow and grow! That is the greatness of man. And in that aspect of his being, man is unique — even greater than the angels, who have no ability to grow.

The word "very" has no defined limit. Man's capacity, too, has no limit. He can grow and grow and grow!

In his eulogy of Rabbi Chaim Elazar Wachs, author of *Nefesh Chayah*, the *Avnei Nezer* quoted the Talmudic narrative (*Berachos* 5b) that states that R' Elazar wept when he looked at R' Yochanan, who, aside from being one of the greatest of the Talmudic sages, was extraordinarily handsome. When R' Yochanan asked R' Elazar why he was crying, he answered, "Woe that such beauty should eventually rot in the earth."

The *Avnei Nezer* explained that it is clear that people of such stature were unconcerned with physical beauty. Rather, R' Elazar referred to the spiritual beauty — the glow — that emanated from his teacher, R' Yochanan. Such beauty is not inborn. It is achieved only with years and years of unremitting

R' Elazar referred to the spiritual beauty — the glow — that emanated from his teacher, R' Yochanan. Such beauty is not inborn.

effort. It is true, as the Talmud teaches, that when a great man leaves this world, his replacement is born. But that means only that there is someone else in the world with the *potential* to become so great. Will he realize his potential? Will he invest the necessary effort, the prayer, the concentration, the obsession to grow and serve God that R' Yochanan did?

R' Elazar cried for he realized that perhaps R' Yochanan's spiritual beauty would be interred with his body, not to be duplicated. R' Yochanan agreed. And so they both wept.

III. Not Just 613

R' Simlai expounded: 613 commandments were related to Moshe . . . Kind David came and established eleven as the basis [for the fulfillment of the 613] . . . Yeshayah came and established the basis upon six . . . Michah came and established the basis on three . . . Yeshayah came again and established the basis on two . . . Chavakkuk came and established them upon one, as it says: וְצַדִּיק בֶּאֱמוּנָתוֹ יִחְיֶה, *"But the righteous shall live through his faith" (Makkos 23b).*

Roots and Growth

THE PURPOSE OF THE TORAH'S 613 commandments is to enable the Jew to become a צֶלֶם אֱלֹקִים, an *image of God*, to the fullest possible degree. By doing God's will, man comes closer to Him, and by refraining from anything that God forbids, man prevents himself from being swept away from his goal. The 248 positive commandments correspond to the organs of the body, so that by performing all the commandments, the Jew refines every organ, until body and soul are united in spiritual perfection.

However, the Vilna Gaon, quoted by his brother (*Maalos HaTorah*), taught that the number 613 cannot mean that those are the only acts that the Torah either requires or forbids. From the beginning of the Torah until *Parashah Bo* — a total of sixty-one chapters — there are only three commandments. In addition, there are many other chapters that contain no commandments. It is illogical to say that so much of the Torah is without any expression of God's will.

Rather, the Gaon explains, the 613 commandments are like the roots of a tree. From the roots grows the trunk, from which grow branches, twigs, leaves and fruits. So too, every word of the Torah is an expression of God's will, so that "everyone with a discerning eye and an understanding heart" can obey God's will constantly at every moment. Thus, every activity in life should be an emanation of God's will, even though it is not technically one of the 613 commandments.

This concept illuminates a teaching of the Sages: Jerusalem was destroyed only because the people acted on the letter of the law, and did not do more than the law requires (*Bava Metzia* 30b). That Talmudic teaching appears in the context of many Scriptural implications and stories of great people who exhibited personal and monetary kindness beyond the strict letter of the law, even though they were not halachically required to do so. But if there was no such requirement, and if people were indeed scrupulous in not disobeying the law, why were the people of Jerusalem held liable? In light of the

Gaon's explanation, we can understand it very well. The 613 commandments are not all that the Torah teaches and not all that God expects of us. There is much more.

To Be Like a Tree

RABBI GEDALIAH SCHORR ELABORATES ON THIS theme. The Torah likens man to a tree: כִּי הָאָדָם עֵץ הַשָּׂדֶה, *For a man is like a tree of the field* (*Devarim* 20:19). Many homiletical interpretations have been offered to explain the comparison. Rabbi Schorr notes that the Torah does not compare man to vegetation, only to trees. The difference between the two is that vegetables must be planted anew every year, while trees produce a crop annually. But although fruit grows year after year, the tree must not be neglected. It needs pruning, digging, fertilizing and so on. So too, a person should be like a tree in that he should strive to condition himself to the point where he naturally "produces" rich spiritual crops year after year. However, he must never be content with past accomplishments. The work must be constant, the "tree" must be cared for so that its crops will continue to be luxuriant.

The Torah does not compare man to vegetation, only to trees.

A person should be like a tree in that he should strive to condition himself to the point where he naturally "produces" rich spiritual crops year after year.

The entire Book of Bereishis serves as a demonstration of how God wants Jews to behave.

As Rabbi Schorr notes in another context — and which illustrates the principle expounded by the Gaon — there are many, many things that are the רְצוֹן ה', *the will of God*, that are not under the rubric of the 613 commandments. The entire Book of *Bereishis* is an example. Netziv comments that the Sages refer to it as סֵפֶר הַיָּשָׁר, *the Book of Uprightness*, because it depicts the conduct of the Patriarchs and their servants, and serves as a demonstration of how God wants Jews to behave. Avraham prayed for the wicked people of

Sodom. Yaakov behaved honorably even when dealing with the charlatan and swindler Lavan. Yosef was the exemplar of virtue even in the Egyptian hotbed of perversion. Eliezer earned extensive mention in the Torah as an example of how even the servants of the Patriarchs conducted themselves. True, there are hardly any formal commandments in *Bereishis*, but it is filled with the "will of God," or, as the Gaon puts it, the trunk, branches, twigs, leaves, and fruits of the 613 root commandments.

Rabbeinu Tam (Sefer HaYashar) likens man in his ideal state to an inverted tree, with its roots in heaven and its growth on earth.

Rabbeinu Tam (*Sefer HaYashar*) likens man in his ideal state to an inverted tree, with its roots in heaven and its growth on earth. If man acts as God wants him to, he plants his spiritual roots in heaven, where they derive energy and nourishment from the will of God — and the result will be that his every deed will be a reflection of the will of God. But if man chooses to ignore God's will and plants his roots in the earth, everything that his tree produces will reflect the materialism of his desires.

IV. Formulas of the Prophets

Devising a Framework

WITH THE PASSAGE OF TIME, IT BECAME CLEAR that with fewer and fewer exceptions, people were becoming incapable of achieving the "image of God" through the performance of all 613 commandments in the ideal manner. If so, was it hopeless? Was there no way for man to unite with God?

People were becoming incapable of achieving the "image of God" through the performance of all 613 commandments in the ideal manner. If so, was it hopeless?

King David devised a way. He established a new basis for man to elevate himself. Ostensibly, he "reduced" the number of commandments from 613 to eleven, which the Talmud goes on to list. Actually, all of his "commandments" comprise Psalm 15 in its entirety:

> *A psalm by David. Hashem, who may sojourn in Your tent? Who may dwell on Your holy mountain? One who walks in perfect innocence, and does what is right, and speaks the truth from his heart; who has no slander on his tongue, who has done his fellow no evil, nor cast disgrace on his close one; in whose eyes a contemptible person is repulsive, but who honors those who fear Hashem; who can swear to his own detriment without retracting; who lends not his money on interest; and takes not a bribe against the innocent. The doer of these shall not falter forever.**

The Talmud cannot possibly mean that David nullified nearly all of the Torah's commandments. Not even King David had a right to do that.

As Maharal and others note, the Talmud cannot possibly mean that David nullified nearly all of the Torah's commandments. Not even King David had a right to do that, nor would he even if he could. Furthermore, he is described as having reduced the 613 to eleven, but most of his eleven are not even included in the 613 commandments. If so, what did David intend to accomplish and how did he do it?

The key is to perform good deeds over and over again, to perfect himself and thereby to earn closeness to God.

Maharal explains, as we have noted above, that the performance of all the commandments enables a Jew to unite with God, to become His image. That is the ideal way and it is the way for him to achieve maximum greatness. But when that is not possible, there is another way for man to elevate himself. The key is to perform good deeds over and over again,

---

* The Talmud explains each of David's eleven precepts, often by giving an example of how someone in Scripture or the Talmud exemplified it. The reader is directed to the Schottenstein Edition of the Babylonian Talmud, *Makkos* 24a, for a full presentation.

to perfect himself and thereby to earn closeness to God. In David's formulation, there are two major elements in accomplishing this: the performance of positive deeds that bring him close and the avoidance of negative deeds that erect a barrier between him and God. By pursuing this dual course, man separates himself from the rest of the physical universe, just as God is completely elevated and apart from all of Creation.

What King David did was to devise a framework that would enable a person to attain at least a significant degree of closeness.

What King David did was to devise a *framework* that would enable a person to attain at least a significant degree of closeness. Does this absolve him from his obligation to observe the rest of the Torah? Certainly not. But David's formula refines a person enough for him to relate to his Divinely ordained image of God, although not to the fullest extent.

Three Aspects

The Torah does not countenance a person who is scrupulous in his devotion only to the God-related commandments, but deals dishonestly or unkindly with his fellows.

MAHARAL EXPLAINS THAT THERE ARE THREE aspects to man's ideal state: he must achieve the proper relationship with God, with his fellow man, and with himself. Each of these in isolation is insufficient. Obviously, the Torah does not countenance a person who is scrupulous in his devotion only to the God-related commandments, but deals dishonestly or unkindly with his fellows. Nor is it acceptable for a Jew to be a saint in his interpersonal dealings, while ignoring the commandments between himself and God. There is another important element in human wholeness. A person must have self-respect and not underestimate his own worth and potential. Maharal explains at length how David's framework includes all three elements.

Briefly, Maharal expounds that the first four of David's precepts involve a person's perfection of himself: his body (as represented by Avraham's circumcision, which the Torah describes as making himself תָּמִים, *whole*), his soul (represented by performing good deeds), being honest with himself and consistent with his ideals (represented by being truthful in his own heart), and being correct in his speech (for man's distinction is that he alone has the power of intelligent speech).

David's next four precepts involve the Jew's relationship with his comrades, his relatives … even with those who are far from the Torah's ideals.

David's next four precepts involve the Jew's relationship with his comrades, his relatives, with people who strive to be righteous, and, finally, to deal properly even with those who are far from the Torah's ideals.

Finally, David stresses that one's life must exemplify his desired relationship with God.

Finally, David stresses that one's life must exemplify his desired relationship with God: never violating an oath, resisting the temptation to profit by charging interest for a loan, and maintaining the integrity of the judicial process by not accepting an inducement to favor one litigant over another. In connection with these three commandments, the Torah explicitly says that one must fear God.

David is speaking of a human being's ability to refine himself so that he can be worthy enough of closeness to God.

We wondered why some of the precepts on David's list are not among the 613 commandments. They don't have to be. First of all, as the Vilna Gaon expounds, the will of God goes far beyond the 613 formal commandments. Second, David is speaking of a human being's ability to refine himself so that he can be worthy enough of closeness to God. If he achieves that, then his performance of the 613 commandments to the best of his ability — even it is not ideal — will bring him as far as possible toward achieving the desired goal.

Rabbi Yitzchak Zev Soloveitchik, the Brisker Rav, was once asked why the Torah never commands people regarding the need to develop good character traits, such as not being angry or greedy, or judging people favorably, and so on. The Rav answered that God gave the Torah to *mentchen*, decent human beings. Becoming a *mentch* is a prerequisite to receiving the Torah. It is obvious and need not be mentioned. One may see the response of the Brisker Rav as an extention of King David's formula.

Becoming a mentch is a prerequisite to receiving the Torah.

Regarding the formulations of Yeshayah and Michah, Maharal explains that there are two essential elements of conduct: *chessed* and *mishpat*, kindness and justice. He explains how the verses the Talmud quotes from those prophets express these two principles.

Through His Faith

FINALLY, THE TALMUD STATES THAT CHAVAKKUK distills all the commandments into one general rule:

וְצַדִּיק בֶּאֱמוּנָתוֹ יִחְיֶה, *The righteous person shall live through his faith (Chavakkuk 2:4).*

Faith must be complete and unquestioning. One who trusts a friend regarding *almost* everything cannot be said to have full confidence in his friend. He trusts *himself*, because he takes it upon himself to evaluate what his friend says and does. Of course, he believes that his friend means well, but if the friend says something that he cannot accept, something that seems unreasonable, or something that will cause him inconvenience or a serious loss of money, will he still have faith or will he question his friend's judgment or — much worse — his loyalty?

When Chavakkuk distills the Torah into one fundamental principle, he means that a truly righteous person has total faith in God.

When Chavakkuk distills the Torah into one fundamental principle, that a *tzaddik* lives through his faith, he means that a truly righteous person has total faith in God. And when someone has that degree of faith, then no mitzvah is too difficult to perform and no temptation too strong to resist. Such a person has an unbreakable attachment to God, and once such an attachment exists, he is automatically an "image of God," and that image will become increasingly solid as he performs mitzvah after mitzvah.

A secondary aspect of Chavakkuk's principle is that a Jew must have faith in himself, in his own ability to serve God perfectly.

Rabbi Tzaddok HaKohen adds that a secondary aspect of Chavakkuk's principle is that a Jew must have faith in *himself*, in his own ability to serve God perfectly. It is a well-known axiom that someone with self-confidence will do better than one who is always fearful. This applies not only to oratory, business, the performing arts, and sports. It applies as well to the service of Hashem.

Formulations such as David's, Yeshayah's, Michah's, and Chavakkuk's are examples for the spiritual leaders of Israel in every generation. The goal is always the same: in times when the ideal way to draw close to God and fashion oneself in His image seems beyond the capacity of His people, there must be a way to overcome the obstacles. In the generations before David, there was only one way. The Torah gives us 613 commandments, and as the Vilna Gaon taught, there are myriad ways to serve God every moment of every day. It is an unending pursuit of perfection. As generations grew weaker, the prophets found ways to make people worthy of attachment to the Divine. Eleven ways, six, three, two, one. Always the goal was the same. Transform a human being into a receptacle of spirituality.

Eleven ways, six, three, two, one. Always the goal was the same. Transform a human being into a receptacle of spirituality.

The Chinuch's Way

Chinuch is following the precedent of the prophets in teaching how we can mold ourselves into God's image.

To absorb them is to fashion oneself into a receptacle of Godliness. Success in achieving this goal brings one to a new spiritual plateau.

WHEN THE AUTHOR OF *SEFER HACHINUCH* wrote of the importance of the Six Constant Mitzvos, he did not mean that there are no other commandments that are always applicable. *Sefer Chareidim* writes that there are six positive commandments and eight negative commandments that are constant, but the *Chinuch* does not include them all in his list. We suggest that *Chinuch* is following the precedent of the prophets in teaching how we can mold ourselves into God's image. He maintains that one who inculcates these six basic, constant commandments into his mind and heart becomes different not only in degree but in kind from one who is observant, but without the transformative effect of these six mitzvos.

The Chofetz Chaim in *Beur Halachah*, at the very beginning of *Shulchan Aruch Orach Chaim*, echoes that contention by listing those six commandments in some detail. To absorb them is to fashion oneself into a receptacle of Godliness. How that is done and the underlying message of those commandments is the subject of this volume. Success in achieving this goal brings one to a new spiritual plateau.

The First Mitzvah

THERE IS A FAMILIAR SAYING THAT THE FIRST commandment that a Jew performs upon becoming a bar mitzvah is the recitation of the evening *Shema*, and this is why the very first Mishnah in the Talmud discusses the time span for its recitation.

Interestingly, *Chasam Sofer* contends that a different mitzvah comes before *Krias Shema*. It is a mitzvah alluded to in the Torah and it illustrates the teaching of the Vilna Gaon and Rabbi Schorr's elaboration that there are many precepts that are the "will of God," although they are not on the list of the 613. The *Tochachah*, or Admonishment, of *Parashas Ki Savo* (*Devarim* Ch. 28) lists many fearsome punishments and states that they will come upon the Jewish people: תַּחַת אֲשֶׁר לֹא עָבַדְתָּ אֶת ה' אֱלֹקֶיךָ בְּשִׂמְחָה וּבְטוּב לֵבָב, *because you did not serve Hashem, your God, with gladness and goodness of heart* (ibid. 28:46). The implied commandment could not be more clear. Jews are required to feel joy in their service of God. The instant Jewish children reach the age of bar or bas mitzvah, they are required to feel this joy in the service of God.

The implied commandment could not be more clear. Jews are required to feel joy in their service of God.

Just as the transformation engendered by a Jew's adherence to the Six Constant Mitzvos cited by *Sefer HaChinuch* is a process that takes time and effort, the commandment to be joyous starts at the beginning of one's service of Hashem and its achievement is a never-ending process. Rabbi Tzaddok HaKohen reveals the source of this joy. It is the knowledge that God takes pride in our service.

What can be a greater source of joy than the realization that God created the world for the sake of the nation that would accept His Torah with perfect faith and devote itself to His service?

What can be a greater source of joy than the realization that God created the world for the sake of the nation that would accept His Torah with perfect faith and devote itself to His service? And what could be a greater incentive than to make oneself worthy of God's closeness by fashioning oneself by means of the Six Constant Mitzvos?

Rabbi Nosson Scherman

Elul 5769 / August 2009

שש מצות תמידיות

the 6 CONSTANT MITZVOS

Introduction

וְהַחִיּוּב שֶׁל אֵלּוּ לַעֲשׂוֹתָן אֵינוֹ בְּכָל עֵת רַק בִּזְמַנִּים יְדוּעִים מִן
הַשָּׁנָה אוֹ מִן הַיּוֹם. חוּץ מִשִּׁשָּׁה מִצְווֹת מֵהֶן שֶׁחִיּוּבָן תְּמִידִי, לֹא
יִפְסֹק מֵעַל הָאָדָם אֲפִילוּ רֶגַע בְּכָל יָמָיו, וְאֵלּוּ הֵן:
א. לְהַאֲמִין בַּשֵּׁם.
ב. שֶׁלֹּא לְהַאֲמִין זוּלָתוֹ.
ג. לְיַחֲדוֹ.
ד. לְאַהֲבָה אוֹתוֹ.
ה. לְיִרְאָה אוֹתוֹ.
ו. שֶׁלֹּא לָתוּר אַחַר מַחֲשֶׁבֶת הַלֵּב וּרְאִיַּית הָעֵינַיִם.

The obligation to fulfill these mitzvos (i.e., the 613
mitzvos of the Torah) is not constant; rather, they are
obligatory during specific times of the year or day.
Six mitzvos, however, are obligatory constantly; they
should not be absent from one's consciousness for even
one second of his life. They are:

(1) To have faith in Hashem.

(2) Not to believe in other gods.

(3) To understand that He is One.

(4) To love Him.

(5) To fear Him.

(6) Not to stray after the thoughts of our heart and the
     sight of our eyes.

(Introduction to Sefer HaChinuch)

Introduction

In the introduction to *Sefer HaChinuch*,[1] the author singles out six mitzvos (commandments) that one is obligated to fulfill on a constant basis. These mitzvos, he writes, should not be absent from a person's consciousness for even one second of his life.

These commandments do not involve action; they are meant to be performed through thought alone. Even so, it is difficult to understand the very premise of the obligation to fulfill the *Sheish Mitzvos Temidiyos*, Six Constant Mitzvos, for how is it possible to think about six different things at the same time? And even if someone could theoretically master the art of juggling six different thoughts in his mind simultaneously, how would he then go on to fulfill all the other mitzvos of the Torah — let alone lead an otherwise productive life?

It would seem, therefore, that there must be a different idea behind the Six Constant Mitzvos.

⇜§ Making Decisions Without Active Thought

How many times a day do we think about the force of gravity? It is quite possible that days, years, or decades go by in which we do not think about gravity at all. At the same time,

---

1. *Sefer HaChinuch* is a fundamental text that elucidates the 613 mitzvos of the Torah. Written in the 13th century, it is most often attributed to Rabbi Aharon Ha-Levi of Barcelona (*Ra'ah*), a student of Ramban and Rabbeinu Yonah, and a contemporary of Rashba. This work, *The Six Constant Mitzvos*, is based primarily on *Sefer HaChinuch* (also referred to as *Chinuch*) and Rambam's *Sefer HaMitzvos*.

however, our awareness of the existence of a gravitational pull in the atmosphere is evident in nearly every movement we make. We sip coffee from a mug, and then place the mug down on the table. An astronaut traveling in space could not have done that. He would need some device to hold the mug (and the coffee!) in place. Even the simplest movements we make require an awareness of gravity. We would not be able to walk, lie down, or shake hands without it. Now that we *are* thinking about gravity, we realize that we would not be able to accomplish very much without its existence.

Although we are constantly aware of the force of gravity, we do not need to think about it on a conscious level. Our actions reflect our awareness of this invisible force as a constant presence in the atmosphere, even though we give little or no thought to it.

The idea behind the Six Constant Mitzvos is that each of the six represents an awareness that we must have. These six "awarenesses" should become so ingrained in our psyche that they are reflected in all of our actions.

Juggling six awarenesses may sound as difficult to master as thinking about six different concepts. We will learn, however, that the Six Constant Mitzvos have a cumulative effect, and by mastering the thought processes behind them, we can learn to behave in a way that reflects all six awarenesses simultaneously. Every decision and every movement we make — from the most deliberate to the most mechanical — can be governed by the underlying concepts of the Six Constant Mitzvos, without our stopping to actively think about them.

≈§ Practice Makes Perfect

One might argue that six sets of thought processes are very different from gravity. Gravity is intuitive. There are parts of the world in which people are raised without the most basic knowledge of science, and yet they are able to place their feet on the ground or pick fruits from a tree without having them float away. Perhaps, then, instinctive integration of a concept is possible only with physical, natural phenomena, such as gravity, but not with the complex thought processes that are the Six Constant Mitzvos.

Let us take another example from everyday life to show that we can keep extremely complex processes simmering in the background of our mind while performing other tasks in the foreground.

When a person first learns to drive, he is often overwhelmed by the multiple tasks that must be performed simultaneously. He wonders how he will manage to shift between the gas and brake pedals, glance in all the mirrors every few seconds, check the speedometer, keep an eye on traffic lights, and steer the car in the correct direction, all the while paying attention to road signs and traffic conditions. A few months later, the same person will be able to juggle all of those tasks with ease. He will even manage to eat, tune the radio, and carry on conversations with passengers at the same time. Unlike the inherent awareness of gravity, the act of driving does require conscious training, but once a person masters the skill, he can focus on other complex thoughts and tasks and still drive safely.

When studying the Six Constant Mitzvos, we must focus not only on understanding how to perform them technically, but more importantly, on training ourselves to absorb their underlying concepts to the extent that they become ingrained in our psyche and thus instinctive.

This does not mean that we can study these six mitzvos just once and be set for life. As we will see, there is breathtaking beauty and depth to these mitzvos, and the more time we spend studying them and absorbing their underlying concepts, the deeper our awareness and understanding of these concepts will become. And the deeper our awareness becomes, the more consistent we will be in reflecting that awareness in our actions.

WHEN THE EGYPTIANS DEVISED A PLAN to enslave the Jews, the Torah states: וַיָּקָם מֶלֶךְ חָדָשׁ ... אֲשֶׁר לֹא יָדַע אֶת יוֹסֵף, *A new king arose … who did not know Yosef* (*Shemos* 1:8). The verse implies that had this Pharaoh known Yosef, he would not have enslaved Yosef's nation. Yosef had single-handedly built the Egyptian economy and demanded nothing in return. His brothers came to Egypt with the sole intention of devoting themselves to the service of Hashem. They were not harboring any secret intentions of ruling the country — they didn't even accept government positions that were offered to them. They would have been willing to volunteer their services had the country needed them, but they preferred to remain in Goshen and focus on loftier pursuits.

There was neither a moral justification nor a political need to enslave them. Yet this new Pharaoh decided to do just that.

Rashi adds a surprising comment to the words, "A new king arose." There wasn't really a new king, he writes. The same Pharaoh who had named Yosef his viceroy now wanted to enslave the Jews. The king wasn't new; only his decrees were new. The old decrees made Yosef second-in-command in Egypt and showed appreciation for the presence of Yosef's family. The new decrees said the Jews are traitors, and we had better enslave them before they drive us out of the land.

What does it mean that the king did not know Yosef? Did he suffer from severe amnesia? Rashi explains that he *pretended* not to know Yosef. But Hashem did not use poetic license in choosing the words in the Torah. It seems that there was something about Pharaoh's behavior that indicated a genuine lack of knowledge of Yosef.

In describing Pharaoh's behavior this way, the Torah is imparting an important message: If you can ignore something, you don't really know it, you don't really understand it, and you haven't really internalized it. If Pharaoh was able to ignore all that Yosef had done for his country, it means that he never really knew him. Had he really known Yosef in the years that he had been the viceroy, Pharaoh could never have done what he did.

This failing exists in each of us to some extent or another. We study and witness things — and even talk and write about them — without *really* knowing them.

> *A cab driver who was driving Rabbi Yechezkel Levenstein, mashgiach of Mir in Europe and later in Ponevezh, related that he once witnessed an open miracle. When secular Israelis finish their army service, they typically unwind by touring some exotic location. After his discharge, this cab driver had gone with a few of his buddies to tour a mountainous region in Africa. One night, they awoke in their tent to hear one of their friends screaming in terror. The friend was enveloped by a huge boa constrictor, which was squeezing him to death.*
>
> *They had no idea how to free their friend, and they were afraid to do anything to the snake, for fear that they would antagonize it and make it squeeze even harder. Facing what seemed to be inevitable, a member of the group told his friend, "I know that when Jews are about to die, they recite Shema. You should recite it now."*
>
> *As soon as the ex-soldier screamed, "Shema Yisrael, Hashem Elokeinu, Hashem Echad," the snake unwound itself and slithered away into the darkness of night.*
>
> *"The miracle changed my friend's life," the cab driver concluded. "He went directly back to Israel, and is now a religious Jew."*
>
> *"And what about you?" Rav Yechezkel asked.*
>
> *"Me?" the driver responded in a quizzical tone. "The Rav doesn't understand — the snake wasn't wrapped around me, it was wrapped around my friend."*

This story demonstrates that a person can see something without understanding it, and know something without *really* knowing it. We would hope that most of us would learn a lesson from a friend's brush with death without having to undergo the experience ourselves. But to some extent, we each have a gap between what we study and see, and what we succeed in internalizing.

In studying the Six Constant Mitzvos, it is important to develop an initial awareness as a basis for the fulfillment of the mitzvos. We must keep reviewing them, however, to gain deeper perspectives that will enable us to close the gap between logical knowledge of the mitzvos and having that knowledge reflected in our actions on a constant basis.

◆§ Why the Need for Constant Mitzvos?

One might wonder why there is a need for constant mitzvos. Is it not possible to lead a wholesome Jewish life and meticulously observe the commandments without having these six awarenesses reflected in our actions?

To answer that question, let's examine the circumstances that led to two of the most monumental transformations that occurred within the world of Torah Judaism in the modern era — transformations that, although initially met with skepticism and even opposition by great Torah leaders, eventually became accepted by mainstream Torah Jewry.

In the years 1648-49 (5408-5409), centuries of severe persecution of the Jews came to a climax with the horrific Chmielnicki massacres. Hundreds of European Jewish communities were destroyed, and over 100,000 Jews were killed. These ruthless attacks left the Jews of Eastern Europe in a state of despair and dejection. Few avenues of escape were open to them at that point: the United States of America was far from declaring independence or even establishing its first Jewish community, and Eretz Yisrael lay desolate.

Then, a young man of extraordinary charisma and great genius by the name of Shabbesai Tzvi began to claim that he was the Mashiach. Many Jews in Europe were swept up in his messianic movement, hoping that the redemption he promised would allow them to escape the persecution and suffering they had endured

DAY 3

in *galus* (exile). Shabbesai Tzvi possessed extensive Torah knowledge and was well-versed in Kabbalah (the mystical portions of the Torah). He claimed that his knowledge of Kabbalah gave him the power to invalidate certain aspects of Torah law.

In 1666, after most of European Jewry had accepted him as the Mashiach and were anxiously awaiting his announcement of their redemption, their hopes were ruthlessly dashed. Shabbesai Tzvi was arrested by the Sultan of Turkey, who offered him an ultimatum: he could convert to Islam, or be executed. He chose to convert.

This fiasco caused European Jewry to sink into even greater despair. Although many people returned to the Torah study and mitzvah observance that had sustained the Jewish people through all the trials and tribulations of exile until then, others lost their faith because of this letdown, and abandoned Judaism. World Jewry was also gripped by suspicion. Anyone who began to express interest in Kabbalah was regarded as a possible renegade who would draw the masses astray, as Shabbesai Tzvi had.

In the mid-1700's, the *Chassidus* movement began to take root. Many secular historians erroneously view *Chassidus* as a movement designed to connect the ignorant masses to Judaism by removing the focus of Jewish observance from Torah study, where it had always been, and instead placing an emphasis on serving Hashem in other ways. This mistaken belief is held to this day by people who fail to take note of the fact that the early leaders of *Chassidus* and the overwhelming majority of their followers were, in fact, great Torah scholars. Although it is true that *Chassidus* appealed to the unlearned, that was a secondary benefit of the movement.

The true motivation driving *Chassidus* was to re-inject vigor into people's observance of Torah and mitzvos. Even among those who clung to the Torah despite oppression and the Shabbesai Tzvi calamity, there were people who had little feeling for Torah study or mitzvah observance. They observed the commandments meticulously, but with no emotion. *Chassidus* attempted — and, as history bears out, succeeded — in creating a Jew who *lives* for Torah and mitzvos. It placed emphasis on *enjoying* Judaism, which, as we will see, is part of *Ahavas Hashem* (love of Hashem, the fourth of the constant mitzvos).

Nevertheless, *Chassidus* fell under the suspicion of many Torah leaders, most notably the Gaon of Vilna, because some of its practices — its study of Kabbalah, for instance — resembled Shabbesai Tzvi's. While *Chassidus* became popular in Poland, Ukraine, Russia, Hungary, and Rumania, it did not spread as strongly to Lithuania and several other parts of Europe, where the *misnagdim* (those opposed to *Chassidus*) fought it successfully.

Less than a century later, Rabbi Yisrael Lipkin of Salant (who would become known as Rav Yisrael Salanter) sensed a staleness developing in Lithuanian Jewry's observance of Torah and mitzvos. He felt that something must be done to invigorate his community, and he founded what is referred to as the "Mussar Movement." The central focus of the movement was the study of certain sections of Torah and teachings of the Sages so intensely that one became emotionally connected to them. Unlike *Chassidus*, *mussar* did not appeal to the unlearned. Nevertheless, it fell under the suspicion of many Torah scholars, who felt that "emotional involvement" with the Torah sounded similar to the ideas that *Chassidus* spread.

In certain branches of Novarodok, there were *mussar* sessions that lasted several hours, during which people would sit and repeat a teaching from *Chazal* over and over to themselves until they *felt* it in their bones. No wonder that the movement was opposed by those who felt that the same end could be achieved by studying the halachic portions of Torah in those hours.

Looking back at these two movements through the clear perspective of history, we are able to see that they were nothing less than lifesavers for Torah Jewry. History showed that, far better than other segments of Klal Yisrael, Chassidim were able to withstand the temptations of the *Haskalah* (Enlightenment) and the many "isms" that became popular in the late 19th century and early 20th century. When we look back at the development of Judaism in America, we find that Chassidim were able to strengthen many areas of observance that had floundered until their arrival. Their emotional bond to Judaism formed the bedrock of their unwavering commitment to Torah and allowed them to succeed in building Jewish life where others had failed.

In the non-Chassidic Jewish world, most of the Torah institutions that exist today were founded or led by those associated with the Mussar Movement. For example, the yeshivos of Kelm, Mir, Slabodka, and Novarodok, which were led by great *mussar* masters, produced many of the *gedolei Yisrael* who rebuilt Torah in America and Eretz Yisrael following the destruction of European Jewry. R' Aharon Kotler, R' Reuvein Grozovsky, R' Yaakov Kamenetsky, R' Yitzchak Hutner, R' Yaakov Yitzchak Ruderman, R' Eliezer Yehudah Finkel, R' Yaakov Yisrael Kanievsky (the Steipler Gaon), R' Chaim Shmulevitz, R' Yechezkel Levenstein, R' Elazar Menachem Man Shach and others all emerged from such yeshivos.

Clearly, the emotional involvement with Torah that was the underlying principle of these two movements was the key to the survival of Torah-true Judaism despite all the existential and spiritual threats to our nation in modern times.

In our study of the Six Constant Mitzvos, we will find that the primary principle behind these mitzvos is harmonious with the principles behind *Chassidus* and *mussar*. These six mitzvos require us to develop an emotional bond with Hashem and His Torah, and not suffice with the mechanical motions of mitzvah observance. And history has proven that it is *not* enough to try to live wholesome Jewish lives without this emotional bond. Judaism — contrary to popular belief — is not a religion predicated solely on laws and actions. An emotional bond to Hashem and His Torah is vital for our continued existence as a nation, and for our own spiritual fulfillment and growth.

TODAY, our connection to Judaism and Torah is being challenged by issues similar to those that plagued the Jewish world prior to the creation of *Chassidus* and the Mussar Movement. Jews throughout the world, and particularly those in Eretz Yisrael, are being reminded once again that הֶן עָם לְבָדָד יִשְׁכּן, *They are a nation that will dwell in solitude* (*Bamidbar* 23:9). Israel is castigated time and again by an overwhelming majority of the nations of the world, and anti-Semitic attacks are on the rise in a world that is apparently rethinking the pledge of "Never Again" that it so loudly proclaimed when the horrors of the Holocaust were revealed. After a brief half-century respite, many Jews once again feel unsafe.

Although the era of pre- and post-World War II "isms" may be over, our generation is faced with moral and spiritual challenges that no generation before could have envisioned in their worst nightmares. Instead of causing people to abandon Judaism in favor of some intellectual movement or another, as the *yetzer hara* (evil inclination) did in previous generations, today the *yetzer hara* has adopted a different tactic. He allows us to retain our outwardly religious appearance, while distracting us from Hashem and His Torah in the most deceptive ways. Instead of appealing to our intellect, he appeals to our emotions, attempting to fill our time with diversions that will leave us with no time to focus on our true purpose in this world.

The *yetzer hara* succeeds when he turns our service of Hashem into rote, and lulls us into going through the motions of Judaism mechanically, with little feeling for what we are doing. This "going through the motions" is very unsatisfying, and leaves us feeling empty. Observance of Torah and mitzvos in a way that lacks feeling and depth becomes frustrating to us, instead of providing us with joy, as it is meant to do. When that happens, we start looking for shortcuts in our service of Hashem.

Now, more than ever, we must find a way to infuse our service of Hashem with emotion and feeling — to *live* for Torah and mitzvos, not just "do" them.

✥ Aim High; Achieve Greatness

Some may feel that the levels of spiritual perfection discussed in this work are beyond us, that it is better to present these mitzvos in a "down-to-earth" practical form. We contend that they should be presented in their pristine, undiluted form, for two reasons:

First, a famous teaching of Chida states, "*Ein davar ha'omeid bifnei haratzon* — nothing stands in the way of desire." This statement (which is often mistakenly quoted as a teaching of *Chazal*) is most often understood to mean that if a person has a strong enough desire to do something, nothing will prevent him from succeeding. This is obviously not true, because many people fail to achieve their desires despite the most strenuous efforts.

Imrei Emes interprets the saying differently: indeed we are not always capable of executing our desires, but nothing can obstruct us from *desiring* something, from *trying* to attain lofty goals. "Yes, it was very difficult — even too difficult — but why didn't you *want* to succeed?"

By discovering the true depth and beauty of perfection, we will at least *aspire* to attain it.

Moreover, if we limit ourselves by setting our sights on mediocrity, we can never achieve more than that. But if we aim for greatness, we can hope to achieve higher levels than anyone would have anticipated.

True, some of the levels of perfect faith, love of Hashem, and fear of Hashem that we will discuss *are* difficult to attain. But when we realize that by applying the principles of the Six Constant Mitzvos in our lives, we can make each moment we spend in this world meaningful, enjoyable, and fulfilling, we will take the time to study and apply each mitzvah, ascending the ladder toward spiritual perfection rung-by-rung.

Let's begin.

מִצְוָה תְּמִידִי
CONSTANT MITZVAH
1

אֱמוּנָה בַּה׳
Faith in Hashem

מִצְוַת הָאֲמָנָה בִּמְצִיאוּת הַשֵּׁם יִתְבָּרֵךְ
The mitzvah to believe in the existence of Hashem

לְהַאֲמִין שֶׁיֵּשׁ לָעוֹלָם אֱלוֹק אֶחָד שֶׁהִמְצִיא כָּל הַנִּמְצָא, וּמִכֹּחוֹ
וְחֶפְצוֹ הָיָה כָּל מַה שֶׁהוּא, וְשֶׁהָיָה, וְשֶׁיִּהְיֶה לַעֲדֵי עַד, וְכִי הוּא
הוֹצִיאָנוּ מֵאֶרֶץ מִצְרַיִם וְנָתַן לָנוּ הַתּוֹרָה, שֶׁנֶּאֱמַר בִּתְחִלַּת נְתִינַת
הַתּוֹרָה [שמות כ, ב], "אָנֹכִי ה' אֱלֹקֶיךָ אֲשֶׁר הוֹצֵאתִיךָ מֵאֶרֶץ
מִצְרַיִם" וְגו', וּפֵירוּשׁוֹ כְּאִלּוּ אָמַר, תֵּדְעוּ וְתַאֲמִינוּ שֶׁיֵּשׁ לָעוֹלָם
אֱלוֹק, כִּי מִלַּת "אָנֹכִי" תּוֹרָה עַל הַמְּצִיאוּת. וַאֲשֶׁר אָמַר "אֲשֶׁר
הוֹצֵאתִיךָ" וְגו', לוֹמַר שֶׁלֹּא יִפְתֶּה לְבַבְכֶם לָקַחַת עִנְיַן צֵאתְכֶם
מֵעַבְדוּת מִצְרַיִם וּמַכּוֹת הַמִּצְרִים דֶּרֶךְ מִקְרֶה, אֶלָּא דְעוּ שֶׁאָנֹכִי
הוּא שֶׁהוֹצֵאתִי אֶתְכֶם בְּחֵפֶץ וּבְהַשְׁגָּחָה, כְּמוֹ שֶׁהִבְטִיחַ לַאֲבוֹתֵינוּ
אַבְרָהָם יִצְחָק וְיַעֲקֹב.

We must believe that there is one God in the world,
Who created all that exists, and in Whose power and
will everything came to be; that He has always been
and will forever be, that He removed us from Egypt,
and that He gave us the Torah. We derive this mitzvah
from the verse, "I am Hashem, your God, Who has
taken you out of the land of Egypt" (*Shemos* 20:2),
which means, "Know and believe that there is a God
in the world" (for the word *Anochi*, I, assumes the
existence of the One speaking). By saying, "Who has
taken you out of the land of Egypt," Hashem tells
us, "Do not allow your heart to convince you that
your removal from Egypt and the plagues that led to
the defeat of the Egyptians were mere coincidences.
Rather, know that I took you out [of Egypt] with Divine
intervention, as I pledged to your forefathers, Avraham,
Yitzchak, and Yaakov."

(*Chinuch, Mitzvah* 25)

Constant Mitzvah 1 — מצוה תמידית

אֱמוּנָה בַּה' — FAITH IN HASHEM

I: The Need to Internalize

A man from England once visited the Chazon Ish. As the man was preparing to leave, he asked what message he could relay to the Jews back home.

"The Torah states: נֹחַ אִישׁ צַדִּיק תָּמִים הָיָה בְּדֹרֹתָיו, *Noach was a righteous man, perfect **in his generation**" (Bereishis 6:9), said the Chazon Ish. Chazal deduced that a person is judged based on the level of his generation.*

The Chazon Ish continued, "Tell the Jews of England that the challenge of our generation is to strengthen ourselves in Emunah (faith) in Hashem."

The first of the Six Constant Mitzvos is: אָנֹכִי ה' אֱלֹקֶיךָ אֲשֶׁר הוֹצֵאתִיךָ מֵאֶרֶץ מִצְרָיִם, *I am Hashem, your God, Who has taken you out of the Land of Egypt (Shemos* 20:2). This mitzvah is often referred to as *Emunah* (Faith).

Since these words come from the first verse of the Ten Commandments, we assume that this verse is the first of those com-

DAY 5

mandments, and according to most *Rishonim*, our assumption is correct.

Surprisingly, however, some *Rishonim* (Bahag and Rav Saadiah Gaon) maintain that this is not a commandment at all. Their case is so compelling, in fact, that the burden of proof is on those who disagree.

When a teacher walks into a classroom on the first day of the school year and says, "Good morning, I am your teacher, Mr. Smith," he has not instructed anyone to do anything. He simply introduced himself. In the same way, the words "I am Hashem, your God" do not seem to be a commandment, contend Bahag and Rav Saadiah Gaon, but an introduction: "I am Hashem, your God; therefore, you must obey Me when I command you to do A, B, and C."

The majority of *Rishonim*, however — Rambam and *Chinuch* among them — maintain that this verse contains the mitzvah of *Emunah*, faith that Hashem exists. According to them, the parallel drawn from a schoolteacher's introduction is inaccurate, because his students need not exercise "faith" in order to believe that he is there. They see him. His greeting to his class, therefore, is no more than an introduction.

Since we cannot see Hashem, however, when He states, "*Anochi Hashem Elokecha*," He is not merely introducing Himself — He is commanding us to believe that He exists.

But this explanation is insufficient. If *Anochi* were intended as a commandment, Hashem should have stated explicitly, "I am God. Believe that I exist." Why couch the commandment as an "introductory" statement — "I am Hashem, your God"? Moreover, it would seem that a commandment instructing people to believe that God exists is either useless or redundant. Those who doubt His existence do not study the commandments to begin with, and even if they do, they are unlikely to believe simply because they read the verse, "*Anochi Hashem Elokecha*." And if the verse is addressed to those who already believe, why must they be commanded to believe?

◌ঙ Knowledge vs. Belief

In discussing the mitzvah of *Emunah* in the very first lines of *Yad HaChazakah*, Rambam writes that *the* fundamental of Judaism is, "*leida* (to *know*) that there is a First Existence that created all that exists" (*Hilchos Yesodei HaTorah* 1:1). It is interesting that Rambam does not say that we are commanded to "believe"; he says the commandment is to *"know."* What is the difference between belief and knowledge?

To differentiate between the two, we must remember that the Revelation at Sinai did not occur in a vacuum. It is not as if 600,000 men, along with their wives, children, and the souls of all of their descendants, were wandering through a desert, when suddenly the heavens split and Hashem said, "I am Hashem, your God." The Revelation was the finale of a process that began when Hashem heeded the cries of the Jewish nation enslaved in Egypt and struck the Egyptians with the plagues. The process continued when the Jews left Egypt, and when Hashem split the *Yam Suf* (Sea of Reeds) and saved them from the Egyptian pursuers.

Before that process, there may have been some doubt about who controlled the world. The Egyptians were idolaters who served the Nile, sheep, and Pharaoh, among other gods. They were also experts in *kishuf* (black magic), which occasionally enabled them to make nature conform to their wishes. The Jews who emerged from the *Yam Suf* understood clearly that none of those forces had any power. They had seen all the Egyptian gods defeated: the water of the Nile had been turned into blood, sheep died in the plagues of *dever* (pestilence) and *barad* (hail), and Pharaoh humbly came to beg Moshe for mercy when he thought he would die during *Makkas Bechoros* (Plague of the Firstborn). Pharaoh's sorcerers had also admitted defeat when they could not duplicate some of the plagues with their black magic. Logic dictated that there must be some unseen Force controlling the world, and when Moshe identified that Force to be Hashem, we *believed* him.

At Sinai, there was a new element: we *saw* a manifestation of Hashem's Presence. We experienced the absolute reality of His existence. Once the Divine Presence descended and declared, "I am Hashem, your God, Who has taken you out of the land of Egypt," we *knew* that He existed. Belief had become knowledge. According to Rambam, the mitzvah is to recreate and live with the certainty we had at Sinai — to *know* that Hashem exists, not just believe it. Similarly, *Chinuch* states that the mitzvah of *Emunah* is to take the basic level of faith that already exists in our mind, build on it and internalize it, so that we feel Hashem's influence with clarity and certainty.

These *Rishonim* present us with what seems to be an impossible challenge. The Jewish people who stood at Sinai were able to be certain of Hashem's existence because they saw a manifestation of His Presence. We, unfortunately, are not privy to such a phenomenal display. We do not get to "see sound" and "hear sights" as they did. Is it really possible for us to attain the level of certainty that Rambam and *Chinuch* require?

⋰§ Are We All Philosophers?

Rambam writes that the way to come to positive proof of Hashem's existence is to realize that there is no other explanation for First Existence. All other systems of explaining Creation fall short when they get back to the first step. They claim to have an explanation for step two, or two million, but they can never explain step one.

It would seem that Rambam maintains that in order to fulfill the mitzvah of *Emunah*, each Jew must be an analytical philosopher. But few human beings can grasp such deep philosophical proofs. Does that mean that most people are unable to fulfill the mitzvah of *Emunah*?

Chinuch teaches that there are simpler methods of fulfilling this mitzvah. He writes that there are three ways to internalize *Emunah*:

(1) Talk About Emunah

When we talk about *Emunah*, both to others and to ourselves, it penetrates deep into our hearts and becomes part of our consciousness.

> *Rabbi Shlomo Wolbe, mashgiach of Yeshivas Be'er Yaakov, once traveled to Rabbi Yechezkel Levenstein, the mashgiach of Ponevezh, to discuss a difficulty he was having with one of his students. When they were done, Rav Wolbe turned to leave, but Rav Chatzkel called him back.*
>
> *"Tell me, do you know that there is a Creator?"*
>
> *Rav Wolbe was shocked. He assumed that there must be some hidden depth to Rav Chatzkel's question, but he could not understand what it was.*
>
> *"Yes," he answered after a few moments.*
>
> *Apparently unsatisfied, Rav Chatzkel repeated, "Do you REALLY know that the world has a Creator?"*
>
> *Once again, Rav Wolbe paused, and again said, "Yes, I know that there is a Creator."*
>
> *"Good," replied Rav Chatzkel. "Then go back and tell your talmidim that there is a Creator."*
>
> *"It took a long time for me to understand what Rav Chatzkel wanted," recalled Rav Wolbe. "Two weeks after this incident, I finally realized what he meant. There are people who go through their daily lives, studying Torah, performing mitzvos — living as all good Jews should — without feeling in the depth of their hearts that there is a Creator. Rav Chatzkel was telling me that I should be sure to infuse my students with the knowledge and feeling of Hashem's existence."*

(2) Sacrifice for Emunah

Chinuch teaches that when we *act* with *Emunah*, not only do we show that Hashem's existence is real to us, we also *strengthen* our

Emunah. Each time we make a decision to act in a certain manner because we feel that Hashem is watching us, we strengthen our faith in Him.

Sacrifice comes on two levels, and the greater the sacrifice, the more our *Emunah* will grow from it. The ultimate level of sacrifice is when a person is ready to give his life for his *Emunah*. The very last breath of a person who allows himself to be killed rather than deny his faith in Hashem will be accompanied by a level of perfect clarity of Hashem's existence.

> *Rabbi Elazar Menachem Man Shach would often tell the following poignant story that occurred during the Holocaust:*
>
> *A group of Jews was taken to die in the gas chambers of Auschwitz. As they were waiting on line, someone announced, "Yidden, today is Simchas Torah! We have to rejoice!"*
>
> *"Rejoice?" those surrounding him wondered. "How can we rejoice? We don't have a Sefer Torah to dance with. The Nazis have taken every vestige of Godliness from us. How can we rejoice?"*
>
> *No sooner did they ask the question, than they found the answer. "We may not have anything to rejoice with, but we have the Creator. They can never take Hashem away from us. Let us rejoice and dance with Hashem."*
>
> *Rav Shach would describe how they danced away the last few moments of their lives, rejoicing with the absolute certainty that Hashem was with them. "All feelings of happiness we can experience in this world pale in comparison to what those Jews felt," Rav Shach would conclude. "No experience on earth can compare to the joy felt by Jews, dancing with Hashem, on the way to the gas chambers."*

Sacrifice does not necessarily mean dying, however. The second level of sacrifice can be experienced daily. When a person has a chance to earn money illicitly and refrains from doing so because he realizes that Hashem is watching him, he is displaying his *Emunah*. A person sitting with a can of tuna at a business meeting held in an elegant, nonkosher restaurant is displaying *Emunah*. Each instance in which we sacrifice for our belief, our faith increases in proportion to the difficulty involved.[1]

(3) Use Wisdom to Build Emunah

Chinuch writes that while every Jew can build his *Emunah* through talking about it and sacrificing for it, some are fortunate enough to be able to use wisdom to solidify their faith. Those who utilize wisdom to build *Emunah* fulfill the mitzvah in the most meaningful manner, concludes *Chinuch*.

Chinuch does not limit the mitzvah of *Emunah* to those who can appreciate the nuances of philosophy, as Rambam does, but he agrees that the most meaningful fulfillment of the mitzvah is through the use of philosophical proof.

However, is there no value in *Emunah peshutah*, simple faith in the existence of God without examining the philosophical proofs? There must be another side to this issue.

⋙ You *Must* Use Intelligence

Sefer HaKuzari, written by Rabbi Yehudah HaLevi, mentions the value of accepting Hashem's existence without logical proof.

Nevertheless, it is *Kuzari* that points out that while all other religions began with a claimed revelation to a single prophet,

---

1. In studying Rambam's opinion, we chose the most common definition of *leida* (to know), which led us to the conclusion that Rambam considers *Emunah* a primarily philosophical mitzvah. *Chinuch's* mention of the concept of acting with *Emunah* brings to mind an additional usage of *leida*, which appears in the verse: וְהָאָדָם יָדַע אֶת חַוָּה אִשְׁתּוֹ, *Adam had **known** his wife Chavah* (*Bereishis* 4:1). This usage suggests an intimate form of knowledge that would require one to *act* in accordance with that knowledge. We can say, therefore, that Rambam agrees that philosophical knowledge of God's existence is insufficient. The knowledge of Hashem's existence must be clear enough to cause one to act in a manner that reflects that knowledge, as we shall explain on pages 65-66.

Judaism claims that God revealed Himself to the *entire* nation. A single person can emerge from a cave and say that God revealed Himself to him. If he is powerful and charismatic enough, he can base a religion on that claim. But it is impossible for 600,000 men to agree on a fabrication. If the story of the Revelation at Sinai were untrue, there would certainly have been many denying the story, and it could never have gained credibility.

> *At an outreach seminar, the famed speaker Rabbi Amnon Yitzchak was challenged by an irreligious police detective. The man claimed that since no one alive could verify the stories in the Torah, he could not believe that they were true.*
>
> *"Do you remember whether we celebrated Pesach last year?" Rav Amnon Yitzchak asked.*
>
> *"Yes, we did," replied the detective.*
>
> *"How about five years ago?" asked Rav Yitzchak.*
>
> *"Of course," responded the detective.*
>
> *"And ten years ago?"*
>
> *"YES!" snapped the detective, slowly losing his patience.*
>
> *"Now I am going to ask you a difficult question," continued Rav Yitzchak. "I know that you were not alive 50 years ago, but do you think that the Jews who were alive then celebrated Pesach?"*
>
> *"Why not?" replied the detective.*
>
> *"How about 100 years ago?"*
>
> *"Certainly" shouted the detective. "They celebrated Pesach 100 years ago, and 1,000 years ago, too."*
>
> *"So when did the Jews start celebrating Pesach?" asked Rav Yitzchak.*
>
> *"When they left Egypt!" replied the detective.*
>
> *"What?" exclaimed Rav Yitzchak. "I thought you don't believe that they left Egypt!"*

It is difficult to think back and envision events that occurred so long ago, but it is illogical to doubt their existence. How could such clever fabrications become accepted by an entire nation and be transmitted from parent to child throughout the generations? This line of reasoning, which *Chinuch* expresses in the words, *"Ein adam morish sheker l'vanav* — a man does not transmit lies to his children," is one of the powerful proofs of the truth of Torah.

But if *Kuzari* considers the simple acceptance of God to be a true level of *Emunah*, why does it bother recording such logical proof? A similar question can be posed on *Sefer HaIkarim*, by Rabbi Yosef Albo, who writes that there is a value to the simple acceptance of God. He writes, however, that you cannot believe a person who tells you that a diagonal line drawn from one corner of a square to the other is shorter than the side of the square. You cannot believe something that your heart tells you is false. You either consider Hashem's existence logical, or you don't really believe it.

It appears that the *Rishonim* agree that we cannot have proper *Emunah* without thinking about it altogether. The primary difference between Rambam and *Kuzari* is that Rambam examines the subject of *Emunah* as an "outsider," going all the way back to Creation and reasoning that God is the only way of explaining it, while *Kuzari* begins its examination as an "insider," accepting the Torah as a given and then seeking proof that it is true.

All agree, however, that *Emunah*, even *Emunah peshutah*, requires thought. One may not feel a need to delve into Rambam's philosophical proof. One may accept the Torah as a given and build *Emunah* through *Kuzari's* proof — but that, too, requires intelligent thought. Those whose faith stems from a need to solve their insecurities or from a need to have Someone to pray to in stressful times have not fulfilled the mitzvah of *Emunah*.

☙ Yes, But ...

We have established that it is necessary to come to calculated knowledge of Hashem's existence. But why is *Emunah* a constant mitzvah? Why is it so important to internalize it, and work to clarify and solidify it every second of our lives?

In order to face the challenges that we confront at every turn, we must make God's Presence a constant in our lives.

Imagine an apparently religious person who is less-than-honest in business. If you ask him if he believes in God, he will certainly tell you that he does. "But if you believe in God," you may ask, "why would you cheat or lie to earn money? Don't you realize that God commands us not to lie and cheat?"

An individual with some measure of self-respect probably won't respond, but in his mind he might think, *I know that God exists, but ...*

That modifier, the dangling "but" that people utilize to justify actions that run contrary to God's will, can be eliminated only through the internalization of *Emunah*.

No one stands in the middle of a busy street and says, "I know that a car can injure or kill me, but I'm not in the mood of going onto the sidewalk."

If God's existence is a fact of life, if one uses all the tools mentioned above to internalize *Emunah* — and a few more that we will discuss below — one *knows* that God is there. And when God is there, there are no "buts."

II: Living for a Purpose

Although the basic element of *Emunah* is to know that God exists, the *Rishonim* teach us that *Emunah* is far more complex. *Chinuch* adds more aspects to the mitzvah, all derived from the verse: אָנֹכִי ה' אֱלֹקֶיךָ אֲשֶׁר הוֹצֵאתִיךָ מֵאֶרֶץ מִצְרָיִם, *I am Hashem, your God, Who has taken you out of the Land of Egypt.*

According to *Chinuch*, a *maamin* (believer) is someone who believes that:

(1) There is *one* God.[2]

(2) The one God is responsible for all that exists, has existed, and will exist, both in deciding what to create, and being the only One with the power to carry out His decisions.

(3) The God responsible for Creation also took us out of Egypt.
   Chinuch adds that we should not allow our heart to convince us that all the miracles surrounding the Exodus were mere coincidences. Rather, we must believe that Hashem performed those miracles in fulfillment of His pledge to our ancestors that He would take us out of Egypt.

(4) The God Who created the world and took us out of Egypt gave us the Torah.

Sefer Mitzvos HaKatzar [*Smak*] (*Mitzvah* 1), by one of the Tosafists, adds one more factor.

---

2. *Chinuch* writes that all of these factors are alluded to in the verse of *Anochi Hashem Elokecha*. The words *I am Hashem* mean that Hashem is the One and Only God. *Who has taken you out of the land of Egypt* teaches that we must believe that Hashem liberated us. The fact that these were the first words we heard at Sinai indicates that we must believe that He gave us everything that followed, i.e., the entire Torah.

The Talmud (*Shabbos* 31a) states that one of the questions a person will be asked on the Day of Judgment is, "*Tzipisa li'shuah* — did you await the salvation (i.e., the coming of Mashiach)?"

Smak reasons that we would not be asked whether we awaited salvation if we were never commanded explicitly to do so. Where do we find a commandment to await Mashiach? He answers that the source of this mitzvah is the verse of *Anochi Hashem Elokecha*. Hashem pledged that He would take us out of Egypt, and He also pledged to redeem us from our current exile. Just as the mitzvah of *Anochi Hashem Elokecha* requires us to believe that Hashem redeemed us from the Egyptian exile, so must we have faith that He will eventually lead us out of our current exile through the Final Redemption.

Thus, the *Rishonim* provide us with a list of five factors of which we must be conscious in order to fulfill the mitzvah of *Emunah*. Are we really expected to keep track of all five of these factors every single second of our lives? We would never get to the rest of the constant mitzvos, let alone all the other things we must do in order to live!

As we explained earlier,[3] the underlying concept of the constant mitzvos is not to reflect on all of their aspects every second of the day.[4] Many pieces of information are stored in our subconscious mind, and although we never really think about them actively, we reflect them through our actions. When a person walks into a room and turns on a light, does he first think, "It is dark. If I want to avoid bumping into things, I had better turn on the light"? Just as one keeps track of whether it is night or day without focusing on it, *Emunah* must be so ingrained in our heart and mind that it is reflected in our actions.

---

3. See Introduction, pages 41-43.
4. *Beur Halachah* (*Shulchan Aruch, Orach Chaim* 1, s.v. *Hu*) does write that one will receive immeasurable reward for each second spent contemplating these mitzvos. Clearly, however, there must be some way to fulfill these obligatory mitzvos without sitting and contemplating them, or we could not lead productive lives.

That might be easy if *Emunah* required only that our actions reflect our recognition of God's existence. But how can we reflect our belief in all of the factors listed in the *Rishonim*? There must be one concept that unites all the aspects of *Emunah*, and it is through reflecting our belief in that concept that we can fulfill the mitzvah of *Emunah* every second of the day.

✑ Purpose: In the World

If there is one word that accurately represents God's existence, His Oneness, His being the sole Creator, the Exodus from Egypt, the transmission of the Torah, and the Final Redemption — that word is *purpose*.

Let us start from the end. Why does Mashiach *have* to come? *We* may need him to redeem us from our travails — both on a personal and national level — but does that mean that he *must* come?

Maharal writes that Mashiach must come because this world is not an end in itself. Hashem created the world and everything in it to enable us to indulge in the greatest pleasure of all: to bask in the Glory of His *Shechinah* (Divine Presence).[5] We can enjoy that pleasure only when all of creation has attained perfection, which can happen only when Mashiach comes.[6] We are sure that Mashiach will come, therefore, because we know that Hashem will orchestrate events in a manner that will lead to the fulfillment of His will, which can occur only through Mashiach's arrival. We await him daily — in accordance with one of *Rambam's* Thirteen Fundamentals of Faith — thereby displaying our awareness of the true purpose of the world and our desire to experience its perfection.

If we review the factors that *Chinuch* considers part of the mitz-

---

5. See *Mesillas Yesharim*, Chapter 1.

6. As we will show in the fourth mitzvah, *Ahavas Hashem*, our sojourn through this world is also most enjoyable when we develop a close relationship with Hashem. The *ultimate* pleasure, however, will be attainable only when the world reaches perfection.

vah of *Emunah*, we find that they all fit into the *purpose* for which Hashem created the world:

(1) Belief in one God.

It is clear that *Chinuch* cannot be suggesting that the belief that there is only one God is part of the mitzvah of *Emunah*, because that belief is the subject of a separate constant mitzvah called *Yichud Hashem* (belief in the Oneness of Hashem). Rather, *Chinuch* is teaching that *Emunah* includes the belief that Hashem had one *purpose* in creating this world: to enable us to bask in His Glory.

(2) Belief that the one God created all that existed, exists, and will exist, both in terms of deciding what to create and having the power to create them.

It is obvious that there must be some purpose necessitating all of Creation.

(3) The God responsible for Creation took us out of Egypt.

The Exodus from Egypt — and the belief that it was Hashem Who performed all those wondrous miracles — reinforces the faith that Hashem did not abandon the world after Creation; He controls even the minutest details through *hashgachah pratis* (Divine Providence).

Just as we must believe that Hashem heeded our cries and led us out of Egypt through a series of events — thereby bringing the world closer to perfection — so too do we believe that He orchestrates world events until this very day, steadily bringing the world closer to perfection.

(4) God gave us the Torah.

Since Hashem created the world so that we can take pleasure in His Presence, it follows that He must have given us a guide with which to perfect the world and hasten the day when that would become possible. That guide is the Torah.[7]

---

7. We must realize, however, that Hashem can — and will — bring the world to spiritual perfection with or without our involvement. He allows us to take part in perfecting the world for *our own* benefit, so that we can enjoy the reward we will receive for our efforts (see pages 133-135).

When we internalize these beliefs and start to view the world through the proper perspective, historical events that are otherwise inexplicable begin to make sense. We learn to view history in terms of the world being moved closer to perfection, not as a series of unrelated events.

Shortly after the Holocaust, a survivor came to visit the Chazon Ish. The man had been a believer prior to the war, but the atrocities he had witnessed shook his faith. He asked the question that many others asked at the time: How could Hashem allow such destruction to take place?

"If you were to see a world-class tailor take a bolt of expensive cloth and cut it into pieces, would you ask why he ruined the cloth?" asked the Chazon Ish. "You would understand that he will create a stunning garment from those pieces.

"During the Holocaust, Hashem shredded the world — and European Jewry in particular — into pieces. You can be sure that the resulting 'garment' will be wondrous."

⋖§ Purpose: In our Lives

An *Emunah*-filled outlook on life is not only essential for understanding history; it also enables us to understand events that occur in our own lives. Once you realize that the purpose of the world — and your purpose as a player in it — is to attain perfection, you begin to notice Hashem's Hand in your life. You begin to view troublesome events as challenges that will help you grow. You no longer take the good for granted; you realize that Hashem is giving you tools with which to advance. You cease to view events in your life as random occurrences. Every event — major or minor — begins to fit into the general purpose of the world. *Emunah* becomes part of your life, filling every second of the day, and then begins to be reflected in your actions.

One book of *Tanach* is devoted entirely to teaching us to view the world through this perspective: *Megillas Esther*. The Talmud (*Megillah* 7a) entertains the possibility that *Megillas Esther* is not actually part of *Tanach*. The Book of *Esther* does not contain any clear prophecies — we do not read of any communication between Hashem and Mordechai or Esther — and it does not record a single event that we would classify as a miracle.

It is clear, however, that *Megillas Esther* is not merely an account of events that occurred in Media and Persia over two millennia ago. The second to last verse of *Esther* reads: וְכָל מַעֲשֵׂה תָקְפּוֹ וּגְבוּרָתוֹ וּפָרָשַׁת גְּדֻלַּת מָרְדֳּכַי אֲשֶׁר גִּדְּלוֹ הַמֶּלֶךְ הֲלוֹא הֵם כְּתוּבִים עַל סֵפֶר דִּבְרֵי הַיָּמִים לְמַלְכֵי מָדַי וּפָרָס, *All [Achashveirosh's] mighty and powerful acts, and the account of the greatness of Mordechai, whom the king promoted, are recorded in the book of chronicles of the kings of Media and Persia* (10:2). Why must we resort to secular sources for the rest of the story? Why doesn't the Book of *Esther* relate what became of Achashveirosh, and what Mordechai accomplished?

Rabbi Yechezkel Abramsky considers this verse to be one of the most important verses in the *Megillah*, for it defines what this book is about. The objective of *Megillas Esther* is not to teach us history. There are enough history books in the archives of Media and Persia. The *Megillah* was written to teach us to notice Divine Providence. It strings together a series of seemingly unrelated events that occurred over a period of nine years. Only when we read the sequence of events as they are recorded in the *Megillah* do we realize that Hashem prepared the cure before the malady: Vashti rebelled against Achashveirosh and was killed, paving the way for Esther to become queen, and for Mordechai to save the king's life, thus placing them into position to save the Jewish people — even before Haman's decree began to ruminate in his head. Had these events not been listed together in the *Megillah*, we probably would not notice the relationship between them.

The *Megillah* is not about history, but about destiny. It is part of *Tanach* because it teaches us to examine our lives and try to see how each event fits into Hashem's plan for our personal advancement. Think about the grand events in your own life: the person you married, and the person you *didn't* marry; the job you accepted, and the one that you really wanted but did not get; the teachers who influenced you. You may start to notice a pattern. Sometimes the grand events are not enough. You will have to focus on the minute details of life: people you met — seemingly by chance — who affected you in some way; a train you missed that caused you to see an advertisement on the next train that helped you grow; a ride you took with a friend, during which you overheard a conversation that contained an important message for your own life.

Such introspection can boost your *Emunah*, as you begin to make sense of your life and the path that has been paved for you. It might be painful sometimes. There might be questions. There may be events that you simply cannot understand. Don't forget — you are in the middle of the story. If we were to stop reading the *Megillah* somewhere in the middle, we wouldn't be able to make sense of it. We should internalize the message of the *Megillah* and use it as a guide for our own lives, and have faith that once we move on to the next world, all our questions will be answered.

> *On Sunday October 9, 1994, Nachshon Wachsman, an Israeli soldier returning to his home in Jerusalem from a training course in the North, was kidnaped by Hamas terrorists. Two days later, Hamas gave Israel an ultimatum: if they would not release Hamas leaders and terrorists serving jail sentences, Nachshon would be executed at 8 p.m. on Friday night.*
>
> *The State of Israel was mobilized in one of the greatest displays of unity since the time the State was founded.*
>
> *To quote Esther Wachsman, Nachshon's mother:*
>
>> *I asked women throughout the world to light an extra Sabbath candle for my son. From about 30,000 letters that poured into our home, I learned of thousands of women*

who had never lit Sabbath candles, who did so for the sake of our son — who had become a symbol of everyone's son, brother, friend.

On Thursday night, 24 hours before the ultimatum, a prayer vigil was held at the Western Wall and, at the same hour, prayer vigils were held throughout the world in synagogues, schools, community centers, public squares . . . throughout the world. People of good faith everywhere hoped and pleaded and prayed for Nachshon.

At the Western Wall 100,000 people gathered with almost no notice — Chassidim in black coats and long side curls swayed and prayed and cried, side by side with young men in torn jeans, ponytails, and earrings. There was total unity and solidarity of purpose — religious and secular, left wing and right wing, Sephardi and Ashkenazi, old and young, rich and poor — an occurrence unprecedented in our sadly fragmented society.

Unfortunately, the salvation that everyone expected did not come. Israeli intelligence learned where Nachshon was being held. An elite rescue team raided the house, but Nachshon was killed along with Nir Poraz, the captain of the rescue unit.

Many people were left with questions, but Mr. and Mrs. Wachsman were not. Mr. Wachsman asked Nachshon's rosh yeshivah, Rabbi Mordechai Alon, to include in his eulogy that a father would like to say "yes" to his children all the time, but there are times when he must say "no." World Jewry had begged Hashem to return Nachshon, but for reasons unknown to us, Hashem, our Merciful Father in Heaven, said no.

Will viewing the world with *Emunah* explain every detail of our lives? No. But it is likely to help us notice the pattern. We will begin to see ourselves being drawn closer to perfection — just as the world took a step closer to perfection during Nachshon Wachsman's captivity — and even if we cannot make sense of the outcome, we can accept the fact that Hashem is bringing us closer and closer to Him.

◄§ Something to Rely Upon

Life can be frightening without *Emunah*. The world is moving at a dizzying pace, and technological advancements bring us live reports of world events that we would not have been aware of had we lived 100 years ago. *Emunah* allows us to understand some of these events, but more importantly, it gives us the sense of security that Someone is orchestrating each and every one of them.

A man once came to the Chofetz Chaim to bemoan his lot in life. "I earn my livelihood as a peddler, traveling from village to village. Sometimes I am away from home for a few days, sometimes for a few weeks. I travel through the bitter cold of winter and under the blazing summer sun. Until recently, I was able to comfort myself in my travels, because I knew that in a matter of days or weeks I would be able to go home, where my beloved wife would be waiting for me with some good food, a comfortable bed, and the radiant warmth of a Jewish home.

"Recently, however, my wife died. Now, not only do I have to suffer from my conditions on the road, but I don't even have the comfort of knowing that I will eventually be able to restore my strength; I have no home to return to."

The Chofetz Chaim extracted an important message from this man's tale of woe. Our journey through this world is at times filled with pain and difficulty. Without Emunah, one can become discouraged during such times. Fortunate are those who realize that this world is fleeting, that every measure of pain has a purpose, and that they will soon be able to return "home" and enjoy the warmth of the Divine Presence in the World to Come.

III: Practical Emunah

We now understand why it is important to internalize *Emunah*, and we know that the mitzvah of *Emunah* includes the belief that the world was created for a purpose. Now comes the hard part: reflecting that belief through our actions on a practical level.

Let us look at three examples, following the chronological order of a day in the life of a Jew, to see how practical *Emunah* should affect our lives.

⋚ Setting Hashem Before You

In his first gloss to *Shulchan Aruch Orach Chaim*, commenting on *Shulchan Aruch's* teaching of how a Jew should arise each morning, Rema writes:

> שִׁוִּיתִי ה' לְנֶגְדִּי תָמִיד, *I have set Hashem before me always* (*Tehillim* 16:8), is an essential principle in following the Torah and in the virtues of the righteous. If a person lives with the constant realization that Hashem is watching him, he will consider his conduct more carefully than if he feels that he is not under observation.

While Rema's teaching applies to every decision we make in life, let us focus on just one practical point. Are we supposed to stand out as much as possible, or should we try to avoid publicity? Are we supposed to make our observance obvious to others, or should we try to conceal our virtues?

There are valid arguments for each side. On the one hand, we can teach others by making our observance noticeable. On the other hand, there is a concept of modesty, of shunning recognition. How should we behave?

The precept of "setting Hashem before ourselves always" requires us to judge on a case-by-case basis.

There are times when we need to show publicly that we are willing to stand up for our rights to observe Torah and mitzvos, and even to risk our lives for our observance. And there are instances in which we can teach others by example. To maintain our privacy in such instances is not modesty, but selfishness.

For the most part, however, our mission in this world is to fade into the background. The righteous Jews who lived in the *shtetls* of Europe or the Old City of Jerusalem in the early 20th century would have been happiest if no one would have known that they were born, and no one would have taken note when they died. They just wanted to study Torah and serve Hashem — to become great without anyone ever discovering their greatness. Being discovered might cause them to become vain, as human recognition will almost always do. They went out of their way to hide their deeds, to be as inconspicuous as possible.

> *A man once asked Rabbi Yaakov Kamenetsky's "hoiz bachur" (young man who assisted the Rav in his later years) what he had observed during his years of serving such a great man.*
>
> *"Nothing," the man replied. "Absolutely nothing."*
>
> *Rav Yaakov would determinedly consider all of his actions in advance to avoid letting anyone see any of the halachic stringencies he kept.*

Emunah allows you to become great — quietly. You feel comfortable with the fact that God knows that you are great, and you shun recognition, unless that recognition will be helpful to others.

↩ Talk to Hashem

After rising with God on our mind, we proceed to *daven*. All forms of *tefillah* (prayer) imply *Emunah*, because a person praying before God obviously believes that He exists. But there is one form of *tefillah* that indicates a deeper level of faith.

The Torah states: וְכִי תָבֹאוּ מִלְחָמָה בְּאַרְצְכֶם עַל הַצַּר הַצֹּרֵר אֶתְכֶם וַהֲרֵעֹתֶם בַּחֲצֹצְרֹת וְנִזְכַּרְתֶּם לִפְנֵי ה' אֱלֹקֵיכֶם וְנוֹשַׁעְתֶּם מֵאֹיְבֵיכֶם, *When you go to wage war in your Land against an enemy who oppresses you, you shall sound short blasts of the trumpets,* **and you shall be remembered before Hashem**, *your God, and you shall be saved from your foes (Bamidbar* 10:9).

This verse is astounding. Does Hashem forget us if we do not blow trumpets? Must we sound trumpet blasts to remind Him that we are in trouble?

Ramban writes (glosses to Rambam's *Sefer HaMitzvos, Mitzvah* 5) that this verse teaches that there is a mitzvah to pray in times of need. Although the Torah is referring to a time of drastic need, such as war, Ramban defines "time of need" to refer to *any* feeling of need. No matter how trivial a need may seem, it provides an opportunity — and a mitzvah — to pray.

When we think of *yissurim* (affliction), we tend to think in terms of painful illnesses or extreme poverty. But the Talmud (*Arachin* 16b) states that a person who reaches into his pocket to pull out three coins and pulls out two has suffered *yissurim*, because he must reach into his pocket a second time to retrieve the third coin. How is that *yissurim*?

The Talmud is teaching that Hashem wants our lives to be perfect. If we are inconvenienced, even slightly, we should feel that there is a reason why it happened. If a person understands how perfect Hashem wants his life to be, he can feel a "time of need" every 10 minutes, and there will be a mitzvah to pray to Hashem each time. You're hot? You're cold? You don't have enough food? Don't complain to your friends or feel miserable — *daven* to Hashem. Speak to the One Who has the power to change things.

Your *tefillah* does not need to be formal. You do not have to hold a *siddur* or recite words from *Tehillim*. Go into a room, shut the door, or stay where you are and whisper under your breath so others won't hear. And *talk* to Hashem. Tell Him, "Hashem, please let that check clear in time to cover my expenses." "Hashem, please make my boss happy with my work."

This form of prayer is the litmus test of *Emunah* for two reasons: first, it shows that you realize that there is Someone to turn to, an All-Knowing and All-Caring God Who can solve all of your problems. Moreover, if you can stand in an empty room and talk to Hashem without feeling as if you are talking to yourself, it is clear that you are certain He is there. You *know* that Hashem exists; your *Emunah* has penetrated deep into your heart.

> The Chazon Ish instructed a bachur to work on Emunah through tefillah: "Each time you need something, ask Hashem to help you obtain it," he said. "If you need to buy shoes, for instance, ask Hashem to send you money and help you decide where to buy a good pair of shoes. After you buy the shoes, thank Hashem for them. You will find yourself turning to Hashem all day, and your Emunah in Him will become more profound."

◆§ Bitachon

If you managed to wake with God on your mind, and you find yourself talking to Hashem on a regular basis, you are ready for the most difficult challenge of all: *Bitachon*.

Chazon Ish writes that *Emunah* and *Bitachon* are similar but not synonymous. Whereas *Emunah* refers to a *theoretical* knowledge of Hashem's involvement in our lives, *Bitachon* describes an ability to reflect that knowledge in our actions. A person can talk about *Emunah* all day and night, but if his actions indicate that he truly believes in himself, his boss, or his money, he is not much of a believer after all.

Once we have internalized *Emunah*, we are sure that everything we own was granted to us by Hashem, and that He has the power to support us without having us lift a finger. Nevertheless, we are not allowed to rely on miracles. We are not allowed to sit and wait for our sustenance to be sent directly from Heaven. There is a certain amount of *hishtadlus* (effort) that we must make, while bearing in mind that *hishtadlus* is nothing more than a requirement we must satisfy, and that our needs are truly being filled by Hashem.[8]

The Chazon Ish helped found a new Talmud Torah in Bnei Brak, and sent someone to America to collect funds for the school. The collector failed miserably; he barely raised enough to cover his airfare. The man was too embarrassed to report back to the Chazon Ish. He simply could not tell the gadol hador, who was waiting anxiously for the funds, that no money was forthcoming.

One day, a messenger came to summon him to the Chazon Ish. Left with no choice, he dragged his feet to the Chazon Ish's house, trying desperately to think of a way to excuse his failure.

To his surprise, the Chazon Ish greeted him with a hearty "thank you." He showed the collector a check for $50,000, which had been sent by a generous donor from Australia.

"Australia?" the collector wondered aloud. "I didn't go to Australia. That check has nothing to do with me."

"Yes it does," the Chazon Ish insisted. "We are required to make an effort to fund the yeshivah, but in truth, the money comes from Hashem. You fulfilled the requirement by traveling to America, and Hashem sent us this money as a result of your efforts."

---

8. *Tanna D'Vei Eliyahu* 15 (s.v. *Paam achas*) states that one *must* work in order to receive Hashem's blessing, as can be derived from the verse, "In order that Hashem, your God, bless you *in all your handiwork*" (*Devarim* 14:29) — i.e., you must provide some handiwork for God's blessing to be applied to.

ꞔ How Much Hishtadlus?

Since *hishtadlus* is a mere requirement, but not the determining factor, one of the most difficult challenges a Jew faces is how much effort to place into sustaining his family, and how much to rely on Hashem.

May a person buy a lottery ticket as *hishtadlus* and go to the *beis midrash* (study hall) and study Torah all day? Should a worker or businessman put in extra hours so that he will have money on hand for a "rainy day," or should he spend those hours learning and rely on Hashem to make sure that he does not need extra money?

There are no definitive answers to these questions. Each person must determine the amount of *hishtadlus* he needs, based on an accurate assessment of his level of *Emunah*.

> *The Talmud (Taanis 25a) relates that Rav Chanina's daughter mistook a container of vinegar for a container of oil and poured it into the lamp for the Shabbos lights. He told her that vinegar could burn, for "He who commanded oil to burn can command vinegar to burn as well."*
>
> *Indeed, the vinegar burned. But why was Rav Chanina allowed to rely on a miracle? Why wasn't he required to engage in more natural hishtadlus? And once he was relying on miracles, why didn't he just say, "Let there be light!"?*
>
> *Rav Chanina knew that as long as a person is here on earth, no matter how much Emunah he has, he must still follow the basic rules of nature. On earth, only flammable substances will burn; a command is not enough. But while we assume that oil is naturally combustible and vinegar is not, Rav Chanina realized that what we consider "nature" is actually a series of miracles that Hashem chooses to perform on a consistent basis. Oil burns because Hashem miraculously causes it to burn; we consider it to be natural only because it happens consistently. Although He performs that miracle regularly, it is a miracle nonetheless. Rav*

Chanina knew, therefore, that Hashem could just as easily cause vinegar to burn.

Are you allowed to mimic Rav Chanina? It depends. If you are as certain as he was that oil is no more inherently combustible than vinegar, perhaps. It won't work, however, if you have an iota of doubt in your heart as you strike the match and try to light the vinegar. You must *know* that Hashem can cause it to burn.

Attempting to light vinegar is a black-and-white case. Most of us realize that we are not on Rav Chanina's level, and that we need to engage in a more natural form of *hishtadlus* in order to have light in our homes.

The question for ordinary folk is not whether to engage in natural *hishtadlus*, but where to draw the line. How do you determine how much *hishtadlus* to make, and when to rely on *Emunah*? By taking an honest look at your emotions. If you have no doubt that your *hishtadlus* is enough, then you can rely on *Emunah* for the rest. But if you are worried, then more *hishtadlus* is necessary.

Rabbi Shmuel Salant was the chief rabbi of Jerusalem in the 19th century. The people who settled in Eretz Yisrael at the time accepted a life of poverty, but did so happily, in order to study Torah and serve Hashem in the Holy Land.

One of the primary benefactors of Yeshivah Eitz Chaim — we'll call him Mr. Gibber — was visiting Eretz Yisrael. Mr. Gibber was not particularly devoted to the Torah himself, but he had a warm place in his heart for Torah institutions, and the administrator of the yeshivah felt that a meeting with the chief rav of Jerusalem might cause him to be even more generous in the future.

The meeting was arranged, and as Mr. Gibber was conversing with Rav Shmuel Salant, a scrawny Yerushalmi dressed in tattered clothing and a dusty hat entered the room. Rav Shmuel Salant turned to him and asked warmly, "What would you like?"

"While waiting at the dentist this morning," the man replied, *"I thought of a novel approach to answer one of Rabbi Akiva Eiger's questions."*

"Excuse me," Rav Shmuel Salant said to Mr. Gibber, *"I have to talk to this man."*

They went off into a corner, and spent 25 minutes discussing the matter. After the man left, Rav Salant returned to Mr. Gibber, who had been waiting impatiently at the table.

"I wonder," said Mr. Gibber, his annoyance apparent in his voice, *"if we would see such a royal welcome extended to a mere beggar back where I come from."*

"Are you aware," replied Rav Salant, *"that the person whom you have just described as a beggar is an outstanding and extremely humble Torah scholar? I could not continue our meeting while keeping such a great man waiting."*

The administrator, sensing that Mr. Gibber was still bothered by the long wait and not satisfied with Rav Salant's explanation, tactfully brought the meeting to an end. They walked away from Rav Salant's house in awkward silence. The administrator began to worry that the years he had spent developing a relationship with Mr. Gibber would go for naught, and that he had lost one of his most generous donors as a result of the meeting.

Thankfully, this story had a happy ending. That evening, the administrator asked Mr. Gibber to accompany him to the house of the Yerushalmi who had interrupted his meeting with Rav Salant. They stood outside the house peering through the window and watched as the man studied Torah with his children, with much joy and enthusiasm despite the poverty that was evident in their home. Mr. Gibber was so impressed with the sight that he pledged to keep supporting the yeshivah, and even insisted on apologizing to the scholar for the insult.

Happy ending aside, why did Rav Shmuel Salant endanger the financial stability of the yeshivah by offending his visitor? True, Mr.

Gibber didn't speak about the *Yerushalmi talmid chacham* with the proper respect, but did that justify risking the stability of the yeshivah?

Apparently, to someone of Rav Shmuel Salant's stature, human benefactors do not support Torah institutions — Hashem supports them. The benefactors are merely messengers from Hashem. If they are not respectful to the cause that they are upholding, Hashem has other messengers who can step in.

If so, why did the administrator appease Mr. Gibber? Anyone willing to live in Jerusalem in those days had to have a strong measure of *bitachon*. Shouldn't his *bitachon* have stopped him from pandering to a man who didn't honor the Torah?

In truth, Rav Shmuel Salant and the administrator of Eitz Chaim were both correct. The amount of *hishtadlus* a person must make is highly individualized. On Rav Shmuel Salant's level, pandering to a benefactor who did not respect Torah scholars was unnecessary *hishtadlus*. But the administrator was worried. How would he replace the funds that Mr. Gibber was donating to the yeshivah? On his lower level of *bitachon*, he was required to make an effort to appease Mr. Gibber so that he would continue to support the yeshivah.

Bitachon is complex. It is the ultimate test of one's level of *Emunah*. A person can easily fool himself into thinking that he is doing something because he has *bitachon*, when in truth he is acting irresponsibly, because he does not have that level of trust. Don't start by working on *bitachon*. First work on placing Hashem before you constantly. Internalize *Emunah* by evaluating your actions based on whether they will bring you — and the world — closer to its purpose. Then work on *tefillah*. Talk to Hashem. Feel His Presence at your side at all times. Finally, you will be ready to express your absolute clarity in Hashem's existence by demonstrating *bitachon* in your actions. It might require painful sacrifice, and it might require you to act in a manner that others would consider irrational. Ultimately, however, such sacrifice will enable you to keep advancing in your level of *Emunah*.

❧ Never Finished

We have completed the study of the mitzvah of *Emunah*, but we are not finished.

Each year we finish the Torah on Simchas Torah, and immediately start again from *Bereishis*. We study the *parashiyos* week after week, year after year, and we don't get bored. Why? Because as we go through life, we grow and develop. The insights we had into the *parashiyos* last year were at our level of understanding last year. Now we are deeper, more analytical, broader, and more spiritual people. If we apply ourselves, we can understand the messages better than we did last year. The messages that we took from the weekly Torah portion last year will be augmented by additional messages.

The same is true for *Emunah* and the five mitzvos that follow it.

As you grow, you should review the mitzvah of *Emunah*, and find more and more meaning in it.

And *Emunah* is a life's work. Rav Yechezkel Levenstein would tell people that he was afraid to stop thinking about *Emunah* for a second, lest he lose it — and that was coming from a person whom the *Chazon Ish* described as one who "feels *Emunah* in a physical sense." We must keep working, keep gaining more clarity, or we can lose all that we have achieved.

But that is not the only reason we are not finished. As we study the other constant mitzvos, we will find that they are all outgrowths of *Emunah*, and that we can fulfill them properly only when our lives are saturated with *Emunah*.

MITZVAH REVIEW

Constant
Mitzvah

1

מצוה
תמידית

אֱמוּנָה בַּה' — FAITH IN HASHEM

In this mitzvah, we learned to differentiate between *belief* and *knowledge* of Hashem's existence, and to appreciate how that difference will manifest itself in our daily lives: when we *know* that Hashem exists, we will never act in a way that contradicts that knowledge.

In addition, we have learned that part of *Emunah* is to realize that Hashem created this world for a purpose — to enable us to enjoy the reward of basking in the Glory of His Divine Presence in a world that has attained perfection. We know that we can take an active role in perfecting the world, and that our reward will be proportionate with the efforts that we expend toward that end.

Practical Applications of Emunah

(1) Talk About Emunah

By talking about *Emunah*, we reinforce our knowledge of Hashem's existence.

(2) Sacrifice for Emunah

When we force ourselves to act in a certain manner because we realize that Hashem is watching us, our knowledge of His Omnipresence becomes stronger.

(3) Use Wisdom to Build Emunah

We can find proof of God's existence in nature, in the Torah, in history, and in logic. The more we study these proofs, the more we will build our *Emunah*.

(4) Shivisi Hashem Lenegdi Samid

When we are conscious of Hashem's constant presence in our lives, we make decisions based on how they will affect our relationship with Him. Among other benefits, this will teach us to shun attention and not seek human recognition for our spiritual accomplishments.

(5) Talk to Hashem

Aside from the scheduled prayers, we should *talk* to Hashem on a regular basis, requesting His assistance in every pursuit — from the most spiritual to the most mundane.

(6) Bitachon

We can display and build *Emunah* by determining how much *hishtadlus* (effort) we must really undertake in our individual circumstances and levels of *Emunah*, and relying on Hashem for the rest.

מצוה תמידי

CONSTANT MITZVAH

2

לֹא יִהְיֶה

Not to Believe
in Other Gods

שֶׁלֹּא נַאֲמִין אֱלוֹהוֹת בִּלְתִּי הַשֵּׁם לְבַדּוֹ
Not to believe in gods other than Hashem

שֶׁלֹּא נַאֲמִין אֱלֹהִים זוּלָתִי הַשֵּׁם יִתְבָּרֵךְ לְבַדּוֹ, שֶׁנֶּאֱמַר
[שמות כ, ג] "לֹא יִהְיֶה לְךָ אֱלֹהִים אֲחֵרִים עַל פָּנָי", וּפֵירוּשׁוֹ לֹא
תַאֲמִין אֱלוֹהַּ אַחֵר זוּלָתִי. וְכָתַב הָרַמְבַּ"ן ז"ל [בפירוש התורה
כאן, ובהשגותיו לסה"מ ל"ת ה'], לֹא תִמְצָא לְעוֹלָם שֶׁיֹּאמַר
הַכָּתוּב "אֱלֹהִים אֲחֵרִים" רַק עַל הַאֲמָנַת הַלֵּב, אֲבָל עַל הָעֲשִׂיָּה
לֹא יֹאמַר לְעוֹלָם לֹא תַעֲשֶׂה אֱלֹהִים אֲחֵרִים, כִּי לֹא תִפּוֹל בִּלְשׁוֹן
עֲשִׂיָּה "אֲחֵרִים".

We are not to believe in gods other than Hashem
Himself, as the Torah states, "You shall not have other
gods in My presence" (*Shemos* 20:3). Ramban notes
that one will never find Scriptural mention of "*other*
gods" in reference to *making* idols, because the word
"other" is inappropriate in the context of *making* gods
(i.e., since we did not make the first God, how can we
make "others"?). Rather, the Torah proscribes belief in
one's heart [that other gods exist].

(*Chinuch, Mitzvah* 26)

Constant Mitzvah **2** מצוה תמידית

לֹא יִהְיֶה — NOT TO BELIEVE IN OTHER GODS

I: Don't Forget the Purpose

⊷§ Why All the Warnings?

Idolatry is the sin that is perhaps the most frequently mentioned in the Torah. Considering how common idolatry was in ancient times, it seems reasonable that it would appear frequently in books written for that era. But worship is no longer the "in thing." If in the olden days the battle was fought between paganism and belief in Hashem, in our time the struggle is between belief in Hashem and belief in nothing. Nowadays, when we read the repeated warnings not to serve idols, we wonder how they apply to us. But the Torah is timeless. The fact that we no longer have the temptation to serve stones, animals, or the sun and moon does not mean that the warnings not to serve idols are obsolete. The principle of idolatry must exist in our times, too.

Our understanding of the mitzvah of לֹא יִהְיֶה לְךָ אֱלֹהִים אֲחֵרִים, *"you shall not have other gods," must answer the question: Why all the warnings?*

❦ Idol Worship: Not Denial

The first of the Six Constant Mitzvos was the positive commandment of *Emunah*, which we defined as being secure knowledge that God exists and that He created the world for a specific purpose (namely, to bring it to perfection), and to manifest that knowledge in our behavior. The second of the six is a *lo saaseh*, a prohibition: לֹא יִהְיֶה לְךָ אֱלֹהִים אֲחֵרִים עַל פָּנָי, *You shall not have other gods in My Presence* (*Shemos* 20:3). *Chinuch* (see title page to this mitzvah) quotes Ramban's teaching that *Lo Yihiyeh* does not proscribe the manufacture of idols. Rather, it prohibits us from believing in our heart that other gods exist.

We will learn that the third of the constant mitzvos is *Yichud Hashem*, the belief that Hashem is the One and Only God. How does the second commandment, *Lo Yihiyeh*, which prohibits belief in other powers, differ from *Yichud Hashem*?[1] *Chinuch* alludes to the difference in his primary example of a belief that would be forbidden by *Lo Yihiyeh*:

> If a person accepts one of the creations upon himself as a god
> — *even if he believes that Hashem rules over that being and its
> power* — he transgresses *Lo Yihiyeh*.

Yichud Hashem requires us to believe that Hashem is the only deity, and that He has no *partners* or *competition* that might be considered to be His equal. *Lo Yihiyeh* prohibits us from placing our faith in any of Hashem's creations, even if we recognize that they — and the power they wield — are *merely servants of His*. Thus, a belief

---

1. Although one is a positive commandment and one is prohibitive, if they required the belief in the exact same principle they could not qualify as two separate mitzvos out of the Six Constant Mitzvos.

that would acknowledge that Hashem is the only One, even though He grants a degree of power to His "servants," would not be in violation of *Yichud Hashem*, but would be in violation of *Lo Yihiyeh*.

Chinuch seems to consider belief in subservient powers the quintessential form of *Lo Yihiyeh*, as evidenced by his mention of it as the primary example of the prohibition. Perhaps he based his opinion on Rambam's description of how idol worship began.

Rambam (*Hilchos Avodas Kochavim* 1:1) writes that in the days of Enosh (Adam HaRishon's grandson), humanity erred grievously. They were so awed by the systems of stars and galaxies through which Hashem conducts the world that they came to the conclusion that Hashem wants us to praise, glorify, and honor those systems, just as a king of flesh and blood wants his subjects to honor his ministers. In other words, the original idol-worshipers did not deny that Hashem created the world and everything therein — on the contrary, they were sure that He was the Creator. Rather, they erred in thinking that Hashem *wanted* them to honor the systems to which He accorded great glory.

Their next step, writes Rambam, was to build temples for the stars and begin sacrificing to them while singing their praises and bowing to them. And again — they did so with the wholehearted intention of fulfilling Hashem's will.

All forms of idolatry — which Rambam brands as "evil" — stemmed from this error, not from the denial of Hashem having created the world *and* the gods that people were serving. Perhaps this is why *Chinuch* writes that the primary intention of "*Lo Yihiyeh*" is not to prohibit denial of Hashem's existence, but to prohibit us from serving idols even if we realize that they are subservient to Him.

✥ Programming Life

Although the original idol worshipers served the stars in order to fulfill Hashem's will, as the generations progressed, ulterior motives began to replace the altruistic ones. In those early years, with Adam HaRishon still alive to guide them, people knew how the various systems that Hashem instilled into nature operated. They were awestruck by the systems and worshiped them, but they also sought to manipulate the systems to serve themselves — and they knew secrets that enabled them to do so.

We assume that idol worship was futile and that idolaters must have been backward and foolish. While it is true that idols could not function exclusive of Hashem — for they received their power from Him — unfortunately, idol worship worked. Idols were able to accomplish things that people wanted them to accomplish. King Shlomo wrote: גַּם אֶת זֶה לְעֻמַּת זֶה עָשָׂה הָאֱלֹקִים, *God has made the one as well as the other* (*Koheles* 7:14). Hashem created the world with forces of good and parallel forces of evil. There are holy ways to cause miracles, and there are equally powerful forces of evil that can cause miracles. Those familiar with the secrets of black magic were able to program the world to behave in the manner of their choice. When idol worship became popular, people attached the secrets of black magic to their idols and programmed them to bring rain, to make the sun shine, and to make things grow. They used idols to gain success.

The secrets that fueled idolatry were transmitted from one generation to the next, until Avraham Avinu began to preach against it. Terach, Avraham Avinu's father, had an idol store. A well-known Midrash (*Bereishis Rabbah* 38:28) relates that when Avraham Avinu was a small child, Terach asked him to mind the store for a while, and when he came back all the idols were broken except for the largest one. Avraham Avinu explained that a woman had brought food to sacrifice to the idols, and the largest one wanted all of it for himself so he destroyed the others.

"An idol can't destroy other idols," countered Terach, "they can't move on their own."

"So why do you worship them?" asked Avraham.

This is a great story to tell little children, but one that is hard to understand. Terach was a rational individual. Why did he worship objects if he realized that they were powerless? Why didn't he accept Avraham's argument?

Avraham was not arguing that idolatry didn't work. It did work, and that is why people worshiped idols. Avraham was pointing out that idols cannot do anything *on their own*. They cannot make decisions. They cannot cause rain to come, just as they cannot fight with other idols. A human can program them to provide rain by tapping into secrets that Hashem created and sustains, but without programming, they are powerless. A god should not need programming, argued Avraham. God must be the Source of Truth, not something that can be manipulated to provide success.

Our brief overview of idol worship should leave us with a question. Granted, we should not be serving gods for our own purposes, but what is *evil* about it? If those who worshiped idols realized that Hashem created them and enabled them to work, why does Rambam label them evil?

Imagine living in Avraham's time, in an area suffering from a drought, and knowing that by bowing down to the right stone, on the right day, in the right way, you would be likely to cause rain to fall. And you realize that God created the stone's ability to provide you with rain. Why would you be considered evil for programming the stone to give you rain?

The answer to this question lies in a deeper definition of the mitzvah of *Lo Yihiyeh* and an understanding of how it relates to the first mitzvah, *Emunah*. According to our definition of *Emunah*, one must believe that there is purpose to Creation, and seek to participate in bringing that purpose to fruition. When we focus our attention on causing rain to fall or grain to grow, we divert our attention from that goal.

This is not to suggest that we can survive without rain and livelihood. But we should see these necessities as a means to an end, not as an end unto themselves. Viewing the necessities of life as an end instead of a means will lead to grave errors. If financial success is a goal, why not utilize any means that can help in its attainment? Why not advance our monetary goals by using the powers of impurity?

If we internalize the lessons of *Emunah* and *Lo Yihiyeh* and consider growing closer to Hashem through self-perfection as our only goal, we have no use for systems that involve no growth — and we certainly do not engage in activities that will distance us from Him.

The difference between growth-based efforts and result-based efforts is clear in the Jewish approach to receiving rainfall, which focuses almost exclusively on prayer. On Shemini Atzeres we recite a prayer praising Hashem as the Giver of rain, and during the winter we ask for rain three times a day in *Shemoneh Esrei*. Prayer, unlike bowing to a stone, is a way of forging a close personal relationship with Hashem, which is part and parcel of the purpose of the world. In fact, the Torah states that rain did not fall after Creation until man prayed for it: וְכֹל שִׂיחַ הַשָּׂדֶה טֶרֶם יִהְיֶה בָאָרֶץ וְכָל עֵשֶׂב הַשָּׂדֶה טֶרֶם יִצְמָח כִּי לֹא הִמְטִיר ה׳ אֱלֹקִים עַל הָאָרֶץ וְאָדָם אַיִן לַעֲבֹד אֶת הָאֲדָמָה, *Now all the trees of the field were not yet on the earth and all the herb of the field had not yet sprouted, for Hashem/God had not sent rain upon the earth and there was no man to work the soil* (*Bereishis* 2:5). Rashi explains that God was waiting for man to recognize the need for rain and turn to his Creator in prayer that rain should fall. Why? Not because rain could not fall without man's prayers, but because man needed the spiritual connection that would be created by turning to God to fulfill his needs.

Emunah should cause us to grow closer to Hashem, to rely on Him, and only on Him. As we have seen, we are required to engage in a certain amount of *hishtadlus* (effort) to provide for ourselves, but when executed properly, *hishtadlus* does not conflict with our reliance upon Hashem.

Lo Yihiyeh requires us to remain focused on our relationship with Hashem and on His purpose for the world, and not to abandon them in favor of solutions to our problems that ignore those goals. Idolatry is evil because it causes us to forget Hashem and the purpose of the world.

☙ Idolatry: Practical, Comfortable ... and Meaningless

How does this relate to our times? While the Torah's capital punishment for idolatry does not apply to the beliefs and practices we will discuss below, the unacceptable basis underlying idolatry exists in our modern age as well.

A glance at modern society reveals a world focused on practical solutions that make life simple. We no longer know how to utilize the powers of impurity to manipulate nature, but we do know how to press the buttons that will make our lives flow smoothly and practically, so that we do not need to think about God. In place of a deity of stone, we have a microwave. Whereas our ancestors had to toil for months, while praying to Hashem all along for rain and successful growth of their crops, we can fill our need for food by ordering it from the supermarket and popping it into a microwave. Most of our children have no idea how food is grown, how meat is processed, or how grain is harvested and turned into bread. The future may well bring with it a system that will be able to detect one's moods, select the dish he wants from the freezer, send it to the microwave, and have it delivered to him in bed.

Who created technology? God. The secrets that led to the invention of the microwave and all other miracles of modern technology have existed since Creation — just as the elements of black magic did — but the latter were known immediately after Creation and the former took over five millennia to discover. The source is the same Hashem, and the problem with idolatry exists in our times in the form of technology: is this what life is about? Have we been swept off our feet by the powerful wave of pursuit of comfort and pleasure to the extent that we now view that as an end instead of a means? Did God create us to have us find a way to lie in bed and be served?

Idol worship — whether the ancient version or the modern one — does not necessarily mean denial of Hashem as Creator and Sustainer of the systems of nature. What it does mean is worship and utilization of those systems in pursuit of a practical, comfortable — but empty — life.

The first step to fulfilling *Lo Yihiyeh* requires us to ask ourselves: are we pursuing growth and meaning, or success and comfort? Are we living for the intended purpose of creation, or are we spending our precious years on earth trying to manipulate the systems that Hashem instilled in nature to our advantage?

The Torah's warning not to serve *avodah zarah* is as relevant today as it was in ancient times. It commands us not to become stuck in a life that is practical and comfortable ... but meaningless.

II: Pragmatism and the Jewish Personality

DAY 16

Parashas Toldos contains an account of the different paths that the twins, Yaakov and Eisav, set for themselves. The Torah (*Bereishis* 25:27) describes Eisav as: אִישׁ יֹדֵעַ צַיִד אִישׁ שָׂדֶה, *a man who knows hunting, a man of the field,* and Yaakov as: אִישׁ תָּם יֹשֵׁב אֹהָלִים, *a wholesome man, abiding in tents.*

Eisav gravitates to the wilds because he knows how to hunt. His decision is rooted in practicality, not ideology — he chooses a direction in life in which his inborn talents will enable him to succeed. Yaakov, on the other hand, does not make his way to the tents of the yeshivah merely because it comes naturally to him as an academic. The driving force behind his decision is his essence: He is "wholesome." As a truth-seeker, he makes his way to the yeshivah, where truth and meaning are studied.

Later in the *parashah* we read that Yitzchak Avinu wanted to bless Eisav, not Yaakov. While we know that Eisav made a determined effort to mislead Yitzchak into believing that he was a righteous man — the Midrash states that he would ask Yitzchak questions such as, "How do we tithe salt (which does not require tithing)?" — it is difficult for us to understand how Yitzchak could have been so misled.

Some commentators explain that Yitzchak Avinu wasn't misled at all. His desire to bless Eisav was based on the distinct difference between the brothers. The blessings Yitzchak Avinu was to bestow were for material success. Since Eisav was a man of practicality, he would be a more appropriate recipient of such blessings. If not for Rivkah Imeinu's intervention, Eisav and his descendants would have been blessed with an abundance of material success to pursue their practical approach to life, and Yaakov and his descendants would have been successful in spiritual matters only.

When Eisav realized that Yaakov had received "his" blessings, he flew into a rage, and Yaakov was forced to flee, lest Eisav murder him. Upon his return home more than two decades later, Yaakov first encountered Eisav's guardian angel, followed by the showdown between the two brothers themselves.

Yaakov "wrestled" with Eisav's angel, eventually defeating him and releasing him only upon receiving his blessing. The following morning, Yaakov emerged unharmed from his showdown with the human Eisav. Shortly thereafter, he received a Divine prophecy in which Hashem promised him: גּוֹי וּקְהַל גּוֹיִם יִהְיֶה מִמֶּךָּ, *a nation and a congregation of nations shall descend from you* (ibid. 35:11).

In his commentary on these words, Rashi first explains the term "goy" in its literal sense — a nation. He then adds an interpretation from a Midrash (*Bereishis Rabbah* 82:5):

> Another explanation is [that Hashem promised Yaakov] that his children would eventually sacrifice on forbidden makeshift altars like goyim (gentiles) in the days of Eliyahu.

According to this explanation, this prophecy alluded to Eliyahu HaNavi's rejection of the false prophets of the pagan god Baal in the days of Achav and Izevel, who had managed to lead much of Klal Yisrael to stray after Baal.[2]

Eliyahu HaNavi challenged the false prophets of Baal to a public confrontation. He and they would ascend Mount Carmel. He would build an altar to Hashem and place an offering on it, and the false prophets would build an altar to Baal and place their offering on it. Each would pray for a fire to consume their offering. Only Eliyahu's prayers were answered: A fire came down from heaven and consumed his sacrifice, with spontaneous cries of, "*Hashem hu HaElokim, Hashem hu HaElokim* — Hashem is *the* God, Hashem is *the* God," emanating from the masses that gathered to watch the confrontation.

---

2. See *I Melachim* Ch. 18 for the full story.

It is extremely difficult for us to digest why — according to the Midrash cited by Rashi — this momentous display of Divine Glory would cause Eliyahu to be described as acting like a "goy." True, once the *Beis HaMikdash* was built, the building of makeshift altars was prohibited, and Eliyahu's altar would have been in violation of this prohibition. But this story is cited by the Talmud (*Yevamos* 90b) as the paradigm example of the concept of *"horaas shaah,"* in which a prophet has the right, on a one-time basis, to do what would otherwise be prohibited, as a fulfillment of: עֵת לַעֲשׂוֹת לַה׳ הֵפֵרוּ תּוֹרָתֶךָ, *It is time to do for Hashem, for they have voided Your Torah* (*Tehillim* 119:126). Could Eliyahu's fulfillment of his responsibility as a prophet render him "gentile-like"?

Perhaps this Midrash is expressing something fundamental about the Jewish personality. Eisav chooses his steps in reaction to needs that arise at the moment. Eisav murders when it suits his needs, yet discusses the tithe when he finds it necessary to impress his father. Yaakov lives according to his principles, come what may. Even the Divine concept of *"horaas shaah"* — necessary though it is in times like Eliyahu's — seems foreign to the Jewish personality; foreign enough to be referred to as a gentile-like act. Perhaps it was the surrender of Eisav's angel to Yaakov that enabled his descendant Eliyahu to fulfill that "gentile-like" directive of *"eis laasos laHashem."* Thanks to Yaakov's victory, it became possible for his descendants to turn an otherwise forbidden altar into a means for a historic *kiddush Hashem*.

In our long and often bitter history, Jews have been at their best when challenged. Hidden strengths are reawakened with the very thought of having to surrender to circumstances. When threatened with forced conversion and similar challenges, simple Jews have become stubborn and proud with a rekindled spirit of *Yisrael Sabbah* (our grandfather, Israel) and displayed incredible *mesirus nefesh*, allowing themselves to be tortured and killed rather than surrender.

On his way to the confrontation with Eisav, Yaakov sent Eisav a message, stating: עִם לָבָן גַּרְתִּי, *I have sojourned with Lavan* (*Bereishis* 32:5). Rashi comments that the numerical value of גַּרְתִּי, *sojourned*, is 613, the same as the number of mitzvos in the Torah. Yaakov was sending Eisav an implied message: I lived with Lavan, but I didn't compromise my standards. We tend to understand that what Yaakov meant was that *despite* living with their devious and wicked uncle Lavan, he had not compromised on his principles.

Rav Yitzchak Hutner offered a novel perspective: He said that Yaakov meant that *because* he was living with Lavan, he was extremely careful in observing the commandments. A hostile environment sparks within the Jew a desire to stand up for his values with even greater diligence.

This leads us to a disturbing question.

Above, we learned that *Chinuch* defines the mitzvah of *Lo Yihiyeh* as a prohibition of the belief in any power other than Hashem, even if we realize that the alternate power is subservient to Him. We explained that the underlying characteristic of *avodah zarah* is the worship and manipulation of systems in nature to find practical solutions for problems, rather than focusing on the purpose of our existence. Yet we Jews live practically and pragmatically. We deal in commerce to earn a livelihood, we see doctors when we are sick — in short, we seem to live within the framework of the practical world. If there is truly something evil about seeking practical, natural solutions for living in this world, how is it that Jews lead lives that are so practical and pragmatic?

⇜§ Living up to Responsibility

To answer this question, we must fine-tune our definition of our purpose in this world. In the mitzvah of *Emunah* we learned that part of faith in Hashem is the understanding that the world has a purpose, and that we can take part in achieving that purpose. How can we do that?

Man's role in the world is to come closer to Hashem by perfecting himself. *Mesillas Yesharim* describes this process as the quest for *shleimus* — perfection in every area of character. He explains that every situation in life offers an opportunity to do so. No matter how mundane a situation may seem, it provides opportunities for growth. Waiting for a bus can train you to be more patient, dealing with difficult people can help you learn to control anger, and so on.

A crucial aspect in the development of *shleimus* is to become a responsible person. Living up to our practical obligations is no less important in the process of coming close to Hashem than is fulfillment of the obviously "religious" commandments. According to Rambam (*Sefer HaMitzvos*, Positive Commandment 8), all aspects of character development are included in the commandment, "*Vehalacta bidrachav* — you shall go in His ways"; i.e., you shall emulate Hashem.

Being responsible includes taking care of our health and our finances. A person who neglects his health or that of his children is lacking *shleimus*. A person who is reckless with finances is also far from *shleimus*.

The pagan of ancient times defined life as the battle for health and livelihood. When his crop was threatened by drought he sought out the forces of impurity to save the day — thus violating *Lo Yihiyeh* in a literal sense, by bowing to elements that Hashem introduced into nature, rather than taking part in the purpose of Creation. His modern-day counterpart has more sophisticated versions of those life goals: comfort and wealth. He utilizes the means made available by scientific and technological advancement to achieve those goals. This is not wrong in itself. What is wrong, and what is similar to ancient idolatry, is to consider such success as the only or primary goal in life, and to avoid the need for growth and character perfection — thus violating the broader definition of *Lo Yihiyeh*. Worse, in his quest to achieve such goals, one may even compromise his integrity.

Jews do not view health, wealth, and comfort as an end. We realize that our mission is to become Godlike. Within the framework of emulating our Creator, however, we are required to handle our health and finances in a responsible manner. On a broader scale, we must take responsibility for determining which conveniences will enhance our lifestyle in a constructive way, and whether or not the need for those comforts justifies the cost of obtaining them.

A Jew takes part in this world in a pragmatic, practical way, but with the understanding that it is a part of his greater mission, not an escape from it.

Gedolei Yisrael, our Torah leaders, have always had the ability to develop practical solutions to difficult situations. Throughout the generations, people would seek advice from *gedolim* on family issues, business, medicine, and all other areas of life. Yes, we are a pragmatic people, but always within the context of fulfilling higher responsibilities, both to ourselves and to others.

The perspective on life taught by the mitzvos of *Emunah* and *Lo Yihyeh* is that our *exclusive* goal should be to grow closer to Hashem. Included in that recognition is that every challenge we face in life is a Heaven-sent opportunity for growth.

Illness, for example, is a way of testing our level of responsibility, perhaps challenging our ability to deal with frustration and disappointment, and further developing our trust in Hashem. The afflicted person seeks medical assistance, works on his character, and prays for a recovery — seeing *all three* as components of his *avodas Hashem* (service of Hashem). When understood in this context, any *hishtadlus* that the Torah does not approve of would obviously not be considered.

Similarly, if one views commerce not as an end, but as the fulfillment of his responsibility to support his family and assist his community, he turns it into a sacred *avodah*. The success of his endeavor is measured in terms of his dedication, integrity, the way he deals with employees and the competition, and his *bitachon* — even more than by the financial return. He would immediately reject any business deal that does not stand up to the Torah's rigorous requirements for honesty and integrity.

◆§ The Danger of Segulos

Finally, let us turn to a more enticing form of ignoring the purpose of the world that has now become somewhat of an obsession: *segulos*. Nowadays, we are encouraged to give a specific sum to a particular charity as a *segulah* for good children; to recite *Shir HaShirim*, *Perek Shirah*, or *Pitum HaKetores* for forty consecutive days to merit this, that, or the other; or to wear a red string that was tied around Kever Rachel for good health.

Is it reasonable to consider that Hashem denies a *bas Yisrael* the opportunity to build a home for the sake of having her say *Perek Shirah*? Is it possible that Hashem sends someone a dreaded illness in order to get him to wear a string on his wrist? Is a couple put through the agony of childlessness so that they should pay for a specific amount of refreshments to be distributed at the *kever* of a *tzaddik* on his *yahrtzeit*?

Segulos should never be substituted for a honest examination of our actions that might reveal areas in which we need to improve.[3] Beyond that, when we develop a deep appreciation for the mitzvos of *Emunah* and *Lo Yihiyeh*, and view every situation in life as a Heaven-sent opportunity for growth, even the most legitimate *segulos* will be applied only as a *component* of our total *hishtadlus*, which will always include efforts to perfect ourselves and become more Godlike, thus taking part in the true purpose of the world.

---

3. A further treatment of this concept appears in the mitzvos of *Yiras Hashem* and *Lo Sasuru*.

III: The Idols Within

In the daily song for Thursday we say: לֹא יִהְיֶה בְךָ אֵל זָר, *There shall be no strange god within you (Tehillim 81:10). Save for a surgical implant of an idol, it is hard to understand how a strange god could be within a person. The Talmud (Shabbos 105b) explains that the strange god in this verse is the yetzer hara (evil inclination). But even the most religious and righteous Jew has a yetzer hara. Is the Talmud suggesting that we are all idol worshipers?*

By examining the tactics employed by the *yetzer hara* in context of our explanation of idol worship, we can appreciate the Talmud's comparison between the *yetzer hara* and false gods on two levels.

"You want to be successful and happy," the *yetzer hara* whispers to us constantly. "I'll show you how." He devises plans for us. First he teaches us to be competitive, to use occasional white lies to get ahead, to push aside those who challenge us. In an example offered by Rabbi Yisrael Salanter, when two people want to see who is taller, they will stand as straight as they can. If one wants to cheat a bit, he stands on tiptoes. An unscrupulous person may kick his counterpart in the shins to make him bend over.

It would be bad enough to see people trying to get ahead in devious ways in the arena of everyday life, but we also see this sort of behavior being exhibited in the strangest places. There are people who will lie and cast others aside in their efforts to get ahead in yeshivah — or even more oddly — to be the ones to head a *chessed* committee. Instead of spending time searching for ways to help others, some people prefer to engage in power struggles to ensure that they are the ones helping.

How strange! What is the source of such behavior? A little voice inside of us that says, "True, your goal is to get close to Hashem and to fulfill the purpose of Creation, but there are obstacles that you can't deal with by following the Torah. Follow the crowd. They will teach you how to be popular, how to get ahead, and how to attain success."

Many of us follow that little voice, that force called *yetzer hara*, like faithful soldiers going into battle. We are worshiping a force within us that declares, "Some areas of life are not covered by Hashem and the Torah. Someone else delivers in those areas."

The first thing we have to realize when dealing with the *yetzer hara* is that he *cannot* deliver. That sounds simplistic, but how many of us believe it? How many people use methods that could only come from the *yetzer hara* to try to attain success, financial security, and popularity? We have to convince ourselves that those glittering images provided by the *yetzer hara* are an illusion. No matter how rich such tactics help you become, there is no guarantee that all your wealth won't disappear. All the popularity you gain by following the *yetzer hara* can evaporate with no warning. The financial meltdown of 2008 left people who enjoyed astronomical annual incomes and huge investment portfolios with almost nothing. People who were honored by the rich, famous, and popular turned into outsiders overnight. The *yetzer hara* cannot guarantee your success, whether financial or social. Don't fall into his trap and let him lead you into oblivion.

Being armed for future battles with the *yetzer hara* is not enough. He has been with you since you were born, and by now you have surely fallen into his clutches more than once. It is impossible to examine every aspect of your life and eradicate his influence all at once. Those who have tried to turn into saints overnight have nearly always failed; some have even suffered from a backlash. Start by examining the amount of time, effort, and energy that you invest into different aspects of your life. Then begin examining the areas into which you invest most significantly, and see how they fit into the goal of attaching purpose and meaning to life. If they don't, then you must work on removing them from your life's agenda. With time, you should reach a level at which all — or at least most — of your time and efforts are spent serving Hashem, not the foreign god within you.

On one level, then, the Talmud refers to the *yetzer hara* as a foreign god because he causes us to believe that there is another source other than Hashem. But there is also a much more obvious reason why the *yetzer hara* is an antagonist. He tries so hard to convince us to chase *what*? Success. As we explained earlier, chasing success for its own sake was the error of the original idol worshipers, and it is the underlying principle of idolatry in modern times. Even if the *yetzer hara* would not entice us to seek other sources to fill our needs, he would still be an *el zar*, because the goal that he presents is similar to idolatry.

❧ An Idol Called "I Can't"

There is one more idol that we must be aware of, one that is so tricky that it is almost unnoticeable. As humans, we assume that there are certain tasks we can do, and others that we are incapable of doing. We can easily lift 25 pounds, but we would not even attempt to budge 250 pounds. We can walk a mile in 20 minutes, but we would laugh at the suggestion that we run a 4-minute mile. In other words, there are things that are within our personal power and others that are beyond us. If we are told that there are people who routinely lift 250 pounds and run 4-minute miles, we will respond that their capacities are not like ours; every person is endowed with his own potential and ability.

One who masters the mitzvos of *Emunah* and *Lo Yihiyeh* realizes that this assumption is wrong. The essence of the first two constant mitzvos is that Hashem is the only source of power. "The *only* source" means that only He can determine when we should perform mitzvos, when we should earn money, and even whether, and to what extent, we should have the ability to move our hands and feet. In the words of *Chazal (Chullin* 7b), "A person does not injure his finger on earth unless it was decreed from Heaven, as we see from the verse: מֵה׳ מִצְעֲדֵי גֶבֶר כּוֹנָנוּ, *By Hashem are a man's footsteps established (Tehillim* 37:23)."

If so, how are we able to move about, seemingly of our own accord?

There is a significant power that Hashem breathes into every human being. It is a small measure of His infinite power. This power is called *bechirah* (free will), the power to choose between right and wrong, and between good and bad — indeed, the power to make every routine or important decision in our lives. Hashem did *not* transfer the power to execute those choices — execution remains under His control. Under normal circumstances, however, He enables us to follow through and act on our decisions, but it is clear that should He decide to prevent us from executing a decision, all attempts to defy His will would be pointless.

When a person says, "I can't do such-and-such, it is too much for me," his intention can be one of the following: (a) I do not have the power to carry out this task; (b) with regard to this task, my free will is irrelevant; I cannot use free will to decide to perform the task because it is not doable. If we examine the unspoken elements contained in such a statement, we find that it might border on the underlying themes of *avodah zarah*.

If the person's intention was that he does not have the physical strength or the personal influence to perform the specific task requested of him, he may unintentionally imply that it is only *this* task that is beyond him, and that he does have the physical ability to carry out other tasks, i.e., it is totally within his power to decide whether or not he will do them. *Lo Yihiyeh* requires us to believe that power is held solely by Hashem; our physical ability is no more than Hashem enabling us to follow through on the choices we made with our free will. The implication that he is capable of performing certain tasks without Hashem is tantamount to self-deification.

The other possible implication is that he realizes that his power is limited to his free-will decisions, and that the ability to carry out his choice depends on God enabling him to do so. He feels, however, that this particular request is so outlandish or so difficult that there is no room even for the desire to do it. Going back to our earlier example, he may feel that even free will does not permit him to think about running a 4-minute mile. Many other tasks are within his ability to choose, but this one is not. This implication is in transgression of the most profound precept of *Lo Yihiyeh*.

Rambam (*Hilchos Teshuvah* 5:2) writes that the essence of free will is that each person can choose to become as righteous as Avraham, Yitzchak, Yaakov, and Moshe Rabbeinu. They achieved all that they did because they *chose correctly*, not because they were naturally destined to greatness. Each had enormous, immeasurable potential, but what made them so great is that they had the will to rise to the highest possible level. Rambam is teaching that if we would be strong enough to make the same choices, we could attain greatness just as they did. A person who claims that he does not have free will to achieve greatness — even a level of greatness that seems too extraordinary for modern times — denies the essence of free will. Why is that a transgression of *Lo Yihiyeh*?

In *Emunah* we learned that the world was created for a purpose, and that we must believe that we can share in that purpose by fulfilling whatever mission Hashem sent us here to fulfill. Since we cannot carry out our mission in a physical sense without Hashem's assistance, our ability to participate in the purpose of the world is conditioned on our use of *bechirah* to choose correctly. If we believe that we are not capable of choosing correctly, then we are left with lives empty of meaning — lives in which we are pursuing success, or, at best, lives of mediocrity. That, as we mentioned earlier, is the modern-day version of idolatry.

✺ Why Can't We Perform Miracles?

According to what we have suggested, each one of us should be able to perform miracles. Since under ordinary circumstances Hashem enables us to follow through on our free-will choices, why can't we choose to perform a miracle and be granted the power to carry out that choice? The answer — shocking as it may be — is that we are unable to do so only because we don't really believe that we can. We may profess a *desire* to perform miracles, but in the depth of our heart, we don't really believe that we can, for two — somewhat contradictory — reasons:

First, because we believe that we are the ones performing the countless tasks we engage in daily, and that there is nothing supernatural about them, that they are like burning oil and not burning vinegar. We forget that we are powerless without Hashem's responses to our free-will choices, and that we could not even lift a finger without Him. We are therefore accustomed to thinking that the actions we perform daily are within our realm of function, but what we consider to be "miracles" are not.

Second, because we doubt that God will respond to "little old us." We know that God performs miracles, but only for holy people. To refute this error, we must return to our differentiation[4] between nature and miracles: "nature" is a series of miraculous events that occurs with enough frequency to become reliable, whereas "miracles" are miraculous events that we witness only at isolated intervals. We suggested then that we would all be capable of causing vinegar to burn, just as Rabbi Chanina did, if we were absolutely certain that Hashem can make vinegar burn like oil. We can now appreciate that point with more depth. When we make a free-will choice with the understanding that our role is limited to making that choice and that Hashem is the One Who enables us to perform it, then, if He wills it, He will enable us to perform miracles. But it

---

4. In the mitzvah of *Emunah*, page 81.

certainly cannot be professed as lip service; if we do not feel it in the depths of our heart, it won't work.

Seems revolutionary? The following two documented stories show that it is true.

> *Rabbi Chaim Shmulevitz (see Sichos Mussar, Bitachon [Bechukosai 5731]; Bitachon VeHishtadlus [Naso 5732]) would relate that Rabbi Moshe Alshich, one of the leaders of Tzefas in the early 16th century, once gave a powerful derashah (speech) on the theme of bitachon in which he said that a person with uncompromised faith in Hashem does not need to work at all; he can study and pray in the beis midrash (study hall) all day and Hashem will fill all of his needs. A simple wagon-driver in attendance was so moved by the Alshich's words that he decided to sell his donkey and wagon and spend his days in the beis midrash.*
>
> *Without a moment's hesitation, he offered his donkey and wagon up for sale, and a non-Jew bought them.*
>
> *The wagon-driver returned home and informed his family of his new plans. "Have you gone insane?" they asked. "How can we live without you working?"*
>
> *"The Alshich said that it is within Hashem's power to provide for us," he said simply. "I am sure that He can give us all that we need."*
>
> *The next morning found this unlearned Jew in the beis midrash reciting Tehillim. This continued for three days. On the fourth day, the donkey and wagon that he had sold pulled up outside his house. The donkey brayed loudly, prompting the family to run outside and see what brought it there.*
>
> *No driver was in sight, and in the back of the wagon stood a large trunk. They opened the trunk and found that it was filled with gold.*
>
> *They quickly called the wagon-driver from the beis midrash, and they began to investigate what had happened.*

It turned out that the non-Jew who had bought the donkey and wagon was a thief who had spent years amassing booty from his "occupation." He had hidden his fortune in a forest near Tzefas. In the weeks preceding these events, he began to worry that people were suspecting that he was the one who had been robbing them for years, and he decided that it was time to move to a different city. He had bought the donkey and wagon for this purpose, packed up his belongings, and then went into the forest where his booty was hidden.

He dug up the earth that was covering his fortune and loaded the trunk onto the wagon. As he climbed into the pit to retrieve some coins that had fallen out, the earth gave way, and he was buried alive in the ensuing landslide.

Without an owner or driver, the donkey wandered to familiar territory, and ended up back at the wagon-driver's home, where the robber's fortune was put to good use providing a livelihood for the believing Jew's family, freeing him to serve Hashem.

The Alshich's students were amazed by this turn of events, but also a bit puzzled. "We also heard the speech on bitachon, and we also trust in Hashem," they said to the Alshich. "Why didn't we merit such a miracle?"

"The difference is that you understood that what I said was true in an abstract, logical sense. He understood it literally, and so sincerely, that he was willing to sell his wagon."

In a similar vein:

The Gaon of Vilna spent many years traveling in voluntary "galus" (exile) from his home. Few stories are known regarding his travels, but one of them had such a profound impact on him that he told it to his family when he returned home.

He was once staying in a Jewish inn in a small town. Inns in those days were usually owned by a poritz (feudal lord), who would demand exorbitant rentals. It often happened that leaseholders would fall behind on payments. Civil rights were nonexistent, and the poritz was free to punish the leaseholder in a manner that suited his (often sadistic) fancy. There are countless stories of Jews who were thrown into dungeons together with their families for falling behind on payments.

The inn that the Vilna Gaon was staying at was no different. One night, as he was about to go to sleep, he heard the innkeeper's wife ask her husband, "What are we going to do? Tomorrow is the day that you must pay the poritz, and we don't have any money!"

"Don't worry," the innkeeper responded. "Hashem will help us."

The following morning, as the innkeeper was on his way out to Shacharis, his wife began to fret. "Can you please ask some people in shul to lend you money?" she asked. "How else are you going to pay the poritz?"

"I'm sure Hashem will help us," he repeated.

He came home from shul empty-handed. His wife began to wail. "We are all going to be thrown into the dungeon."

"I'm not worried," her husband responded. "Let's eat breakfast."

*She was in no mood for food, but she served him nonetheless. When he finished eating, he recited Bircas HaMazon (Grace After Meals) with intense concentration, focusing specifically on the words, "*וּבְטוּבוֹ הַגָּדוֹל תָּמִיד לֹא חָסַר לָנוּ*, Through His great goodness, we have never lacked." When he finished, he put on his hat and coat, and began to walk out the door.*

"Where are you going?" his wife asked.

"I am going to the poritz," he responded. "You said that today was the day that we must pay the rent."

"But you don't have any money!" she cried. "How can you face the poritz?"

"Hashem will help me," he said.

Upon beholding the sight of a simple Jew with such uncompromising faith in Hashem, the Vilna Gaon was certain that

Hashem would indeed help him, and he decided to follow to see how the scenario would play itself out.

The man walked to the poritz's sprawling estate and knocked on the door of the mansion. A butler came to the door and said, "You'll have to wait. A poritz from a neighboring township is visiting, and they can't be disturbed."

The Jew sat down on a rock and waited. A while later, the poritz from the neighboring township walked out of the mansion, and the Jew rose and began walking to the door. The poritz stopped him and said, "I need a favor from you. I came to purchase a certain piece of land from your poritz, but I wanted to buy it at a bargain price. The negotiations got extremely intense, and I swore that I would not go beyond a certain price. I figured that your poritz would capitulate, but he didn't.

"The truth is that I really need that piece of land, and I am willing to take it at the price he demanded, but I am embarrassed to go back and give in.

"I know that you Jews are trustworthy," he said, as he reached into his pocket and took out a large bag of money. "Take this and buy the field without telling him it is for me. The remainder of the money in the bag will be your commission for orchestrating the deal."

The Jew agreed. He went inside, engaged the poritz in conversation and negotiated shrewdly to make it seem as though he were purchasing the field for himself. When the contract was signed, he paid the poritz with the money from the bag. The rest of the money — his commission — covered the full debt that he owed the poritz for his inn.

The idol of "I Can't" is the most difficult one to destroy. Start by thinking about the tasks you carry out naturally each day, and stop believing in your own ability to perform those tasks. Teach yourself to watch your body at work while remembering that you are not actually accomplishing anything except for exercising free will. Grow in your appreciation of your ability to make choices, while increasing your feeling of helplessness to do anything beyond exercising God's gift of free will.

When you succeed in doing this, you, too, will become worthy of miracles.

MITZVAH REVIEW

<table>
<tr><td>Constant
Mitzvah</td><td>2</td><td>מצוה
תמידית</td></tr>
</table>

לֹא יִהְיֶה — NOT TO BELIEVE IN OTHER GODS

Lo yihiyeh lecha elohim acheirim is a prohibition against idolatry. *Chinuch* explains that the primary violation of this prohibition is to attribute power to any source other than Hashem.

We determined that the underlying principle of idolatry is to worship and manipulate systems in nature to provide a practical but meaningless life, rather than focusing on the true purpose of the world.

In addition, we fine-tuned our understanding of our purpose in this world, explaining that we were created to attain *shleimus* (perfection) in all areas of character. Success in attaining *shleimus* is the only true end, and all goals — financial success, health, etc. — are means to that end. Realizing that all circumstances in life provide opportunities for self-perfection allows us to engage in the pragmatic, practical aspects of living, while pursuing the true purpose of this world at the same time.

This understanding enables us to interpret *Lo Yihiyeh* as a constant mitzvah that pertains to our times on several levels:

(1) It prohibits us from abandoning the pursuit of meaning and purpose in favor of a meaningless existence.

(2) It explains why following the *"el zar"* — the *yetzer hara* — is considered idolatry:

    (a) The *yetzer hara* tries to convince us that if we follow Hashem's laws too closely, we won't be successful, thus causing us to believe that some other force holds the keys to success.

    (b) Even when the *yetzer hara* allows us to follow Hashem's laws, he tries to make us view material success as an end instead of as a means, which can cause us to abandon our true purpose in the world.

(3) Belief in one's own power to carry out tasks rather than attributing that power to God may also be a transgression of *Lo Yihiyeh*.

(4) One who denies his own freedom of choice (*bechirah*) insinuates that there is no true purpose to the world, for we cannot attain perfection if we do not have the power to choose correctly.

Practical Applications of Lo Yihiyeh

(1) Of Ends and Means

Maintain a constant awareness of our only true goal: to have a part in realizing the purpose of the world by perfecting ourselves. Be sure to view all areas of material success as means to that end.

(2) Pursue Meaning, not Banal Existence

Identify each circumstance in life as an opportunity for spiritual perfection. Undertake each endeavor not for its own sake, but as part of a total effort to grow closer to Hashem.

Seek solutions to problems in daily living that will bring spiritual growth, not just material success.

(3) Remembering the Limits, and the Lack Thereof

Train yourself to realize that Hashem retains all the power, and that human power is limited to the proper use of *bechirah*.

Additive Effect of Lo Yihiyeh

Emunah requires us to maintain a constant awareness of the facts that Hashem created the world for a purpose, and that we can take part in that purpose.

Lo Yihiyeh adds an awareness that the true purpose of the world should be our *only* pursuit; we should not abandon it in favor of meaningless existence.

מִצְוָה תְּמִידִי

CONSTANT MITZVAH

3

יִחוּד ה׳

Hashem's Oneness

מִצְוַת יִחוּד ה׳
To believe that Hashem is One

שֶׁנִּצְטַוֵּינוּ לְהַאֲמִין כִּי הַשֵּׁם יִתְבָּרֵךְ הוּא הַפּוֹעֵל כָּל הַמְּצִיאוּת אֲדוֹן
הַכֹּל, אֶחָד, בְּלִי שׁוּם שִׁיתּוּף, שֶׁנֶּאֱמַר [דברים ו, ד], שְׁמַע יִשְׂרָאֵל
ה׳ אֱלֹהֵינוּ ה׳ אֶחָד, וְזוֹ מִצְוַת עֲשֵׂה הִיא, אֵינָהּ הַגָּדָה, אֲבָל פֵּירוּשׁ
שְׁמַע כְּלוֹמַר קַבֵּל מִמֶּנִּי דָּבָר זֶה וְדָעֵהוּ וְהַאֲמֵן בּוֹ כִּי ה׳ שֶׁהוּא
אֱלֹהֵינוּ אֶחָד הוּא. וְהָרְאָיָה שֶׁזּוֹ הִיא מִצְוַת עֲשֵׂה, אֲמָרָם זִכְרוֹנָם
לִבְרָכָה תָּמִיד בַּמִּדְרָשִׁים עַל מְנָת לְיַחֵד שְׁמוֹ, כְּדֵי לְקַבֵּל עָלָיו
מַלְכוּת שָׁמַיִם, כְּלוֹמַר הַהוֹדָאָה בַּיִּחוּד וְהָאֱמוּנָה.

We are commanded to understand that Hashem,
blessed is He, is the Cause for all that exists,
the Master of all, the One and Only, without any
partnership whatsoever, as the verse states, "Hear, O
Israel, Hashem, our God, Hashem *is One*" (*Devarim*
6:4). This verse is a commandment, not merely a
declaration. The definition of *Shema* is, therefore,
"Accept from me, know, and believe, that Hashem, Who
is our God, is One."

It is clear from Midrashic sources that this is a
commandment, for *Chazal* frequently say that one
should unify Hashem's Name, thus accepting upon
himself the yoke of Heaven — i.e., the declaration of
the Unity [of Hashem] and the faith in it.

(*Chinuch, Mitzvah* 417)

3

מצוה
תמידית

יְחוּד ה' — HASHEM'S ONENESS

I: One Source for Everything

When World War II ended, thousands of Jewish children were in Christian orphanages across Europe. Nearly all of the parents who had placed their children in the care of priests and nuns to protect them from the impending doom had not survived the war, and no one remained to claim the orphans. Many of the children were so young at the outset of the war that they had few memories of family or Judaism. Rabbi Eliezer Silver, President of the Union of Orthodox Rabbis of the United States and Canada, traveled to Europe to try to find such children and bring them back to Judaism. The priests and nuns often denied that there were Jewish children in their institutions, and tried to send him off empty-handed. Rabbi Silver, traveling in the uniform of a U.S. Army colonel, demanded the right to visit the dining room. Once there, he would call out the words: "Shema Yisrael, Hashem Elokeinu …" In almost every orphanage, children, stirred by a memory deeply ingrained from birth, would join him in the chant of, "Hashem Echad."

ᴥ§ Twice a Day, or Constant?

The source for *Yichud Hashem*, the third of the constant mitzvos, is the verse: שְׁמַע יִשְׂרָאֵל ה׳ אֱלֹקֵינוּ ה׳ אֶחָד, *Hear, O Israel: Hashem is our God, Hashem is the One and Only* (*Devarim* 6:4).

Rambam (Introduction to *Commentary on the Mishnah*) writes that humans are superior to other creatures in only one aspect: they are able to attain the wisdom necessary to understand the Oneness of Hashem.[1] The greatest achievement of human intelligence is to attain clarity in the Oneness of God! Clearly, then, we are about to embark on a study of a fundamental mitzvah.

The first and most obvious question that comes to mind is why *Yichud Hashem* is classified as a constant mitzvah. *Shema Yisrael* is indeed the "pledge of allegiance" of the Jewish people — and we aspire to have these words on our lips as we die — but we are commanded to recite the chapters of *Shema* and declare the Oneness of Hashem twice a day. Why, then, does *Chinuch* classify it as one of the constant mitzvos?

Furthermore, in *Emunah* we established that God exists and created the world for one purpose, and in *Lo Yihiyeh* we added that no other force — even one subservient to Him — could contain any independent power. What are we adding with the mitzvah of *Yichud Hashem*?

In order to find answers to these questions and appreciate the depth of this mitzvah, we must first define the statement that *Hashem Elokeinu Hashem Echad*.

---

1. On a basic level, the Oneness of Hashem means that although there are manifestations of God's Presence in our lives that seem to differ sharply from one another, they all come from *One Source*. *Ohr Gedalyahu* compares this concept to light being diffused by a prism. We see many colors emanating from a prism, but we realize that all those colors are produced from only one ray of light. So too, the perception that makes it seem as though we are being controlled by different attributes at different times — Divine Kindness, Judgment, Mercy, Anger, to name a few — lies in *our* inability as mortals to perceive the harmony in Hashem's ways. Hashem is One; it is we who fail to understand His Oneness.

✑ One Mitzvah; Four Parts

There are four points that we can derive from the verse, *Hashem is our God, Hashem is One*. Each of the four is valid, but only one of them explains why *Yichud Hashem* is a constant mitzvah.

(1) There is one God.

One and not what? Two, three, or fifty? While certainly valid, such a definition would limit the mitzvah of *Yichud Hashem* to being a positive form of *Lo Yihiyeh*.[2] In addition, polytheism does not seem to be an issue that plagues people to the extent that the Torah must command us to recite this verse twice daily and as our souls depart for the World of Truth. Furthermore, it seems ridiculous that the crowning glory of human intelligence is the ability to see beyond the foolishness of multiple deities. There must be some aspect of the mitzvah that is more challenging.

(2) Hashem is One [i.e., not composed of different parts].

Rambam writes that each Jew must understand that Hashem is qualitatively different from everything else we know. When we describe Him as big, strong, powerful, and holy, we attribute to Him qualities that we are able to grasp, but that don't do justice to Him. Hashem is not a gigantic being composed of different parts, but an Infinite Being that we cannot comprehend.

This is a valid aspect of the mitzvah of *Yichud Hashem*, and since Rambam includes it in his definition of the mitzvah, we are required to grasp the deep, philosophical difference between finite beings and the Infinite One in order to fulfill this mitzvah properly. It is doubtful, however, that we would be required to walk around constantly contemplating the difference between the finite and the infinite.

(3) There is no other Infinite Being.

Since Hashem is infinite, no other being can be like Him.

---

2. As we have pointed out in previous mitzvos, in order to qualify as a constant mitzvah — i.e., one that we should be thinking about every second of our lives — a mitzvah must have some unique characteristic over the others.

This, too, is a deep philosophical point that is important to understand, but can hardly be the primary focus of the constant mitzvah.

(4) Hashem is all that exists.

This is a difficult point to describe in philosophical terms. If Hashem is all that truly exists, then what are houses, cars, tables, and flowers? Furthermore, what are we — figments of imagination?

In reality, what it means is that all finite existence is a manifestation of Hashem's will. Everything that we interact or contend with — whether tangible or conceptual — must come from Hashem.

This part of *Yichud Hashem* may sound as technical as the others — and when dealt with in the philosophical realm, it may be.[3]

---

3. The philosophical background for this mitzvah is discussed in the classic works of Torah thought and Kabbalah and is beyond the scope of this work. We present only what is essential for a basic understanding of the underlying principle of *Yichud Hashem*.

Before Creation, all that existed was Hashem. The Rambam, at the beginning of *Hilchos Yesodei HaTorah*, writes that all of Creation exists only as part of Hashem; it has no independent existence of its own. In reality, then, relatively little has changed since Creation. The universe came into existence only as a manifestation of His will, and it is still only a manifestation of His will. Until this very day — and this concept is nearly impossible for human intelligence to fathom — Hashem is still all that exists.

Nevertheless, He has granted us a certain level of autonomy. Autonomy, first of all, in perception: He created us — and everything in the universe — with shape, form, geographical characteristics, human and animal organs, and so on, so that we no longer perceive ourselves as emanations of the Infinite One, but as individual, finite beings. Along with that perception of autonomy, Hashem granted us *bechirah* (free will), enabling us to decide for ourselves what we will do. In most cases He also grants us the ability to act upon our decisions (see pages 110-112). But the Source of our existence has never changed. Everything always has been, and always will be, an emanation of Godliness. The challenge of being placed into a physical body is that our perception of our autonomy has become so ingrained in our psyche that it is very difficult to see past it, but we do have the capacity to do so.

Why did Hashem grant us autonomy?

Mesillas Yesharim writes that the purpose of Creation was to enable us to *earn* the pleasure of *d'veikus b'Hashem* (cleaving to Hashem) and draw spiritual pleasure from the Divine Presence. One of the ways we can earn that pleasure is by recognizing the true Existence and recognizing that we are truly part of It. That does not mean that we should see only Hashem when we look at material, physical things. When we look at a person we should see a person, and when we look at a table we

But in the practical, day-to-day application — the level at which it is classified as a constant mitzvah — it can be easily understood.

Easily *understood* — but extremely difficult to implement.

✑ *Everything* Comes From Hashem

In practical terms, *Yichud Hashem* requires us to recognize that everything we deal with in life comes from Hashem, and that the challenges we face do not come from external sources. We will explain this concept by examining the challenge most frequently associated with a perceived "other side" — evil.

Early philosophers felt that it was unlikely that the same God Who created heaven, earth, and the perfect systems of nature could also be responsible for all of the pain and suffering in the world. They came to the conclusion that there are two forces, one of good and one of evil, and that they constantly wage war via emissaries in this world. Good people are messengers of the God of good, and sadists and tyrants are messengers of some other force.

Some philosophers felt that a combination of the two forces exists *within* each person. The drive toward kindness is supplied by the God of good, and the temptation toward evil comes from the other force.

Hashem Elokeinu Hashem Echad means that both are false; there is only one God, Who is responsible for both good and what we identify as evil.

---

should see a table. If we begin to look at everything in the world as a manifestation of Hashem's will, we will be paralyzed by feelings of inadequacy. What are we and what can we accomplish? Instead, we should strive to realize that everything we see is really an aspect of Hashem transformed miraculously into illusory independent beings so that we can face the challenge of perceiving that there are things that seem external to Him, and then slowly learn to identify them as part of the True Existence, Hashem. The more we overcome the superficial perception and recognize with increasing clarity that there is nothing other than Hashem, the more pleasurable life becomes. The reward for overcoming the perception of autonomy will be in the World to Come, where we will cleave to Hashem with the absolute clarity that we were always a part of Him.

The second approach — that both forces exist in every person — is the issue that we are more likely to grapple with nowadays. We feel mixed messages being sent to us from *within*. It seems as though "good forces" and equal or more powerful "bad forces" compete for our time and energy. On one hand, we want to find meaning in life. We want to grow. We want to take religion and spirituality seriously. At the same time, however, we feel some force pulling us toward instant gratification — toward a carefree life of fun and games. We come to the conclusion that living meaningfully requires painful sacrifice. We resign ourselves to the fact that as soon as we perfect one area of life, we will find another one to struggle with. We think that if we really want to be perfect, we must be willing to forgo all the pleasures offered by the other force.

We would really like to achieve both. In planning our long-term goals, we search for meaning. Long-term goals always focus on concepts that we truly believe in, on ideals and deeds that we want to be remembered for. In the short term, however, we would like some slack. We want breaks from time to time. We need time to free ourselves from our conscience so that we can enjoy some instant fun.

The mixed messages often lead to a certain duality in which we focus on long-term goals when we feel that we are dealing with major, life-altering decisions, such as which neighborhood to live in or to which schools to send our children. But when it comes to minor decisions, such as where to vacation or which forms of entertainment we can participate in, we feel an urge to engage in some temporary pleasure, and we don't think of the big picture. We know that we believe in Hashem and that we want to live for a higher purpose, but we are overwhelmed by the "other force" signaling us to take some time off to enjoy the moment. And that force convinces us that we are not forfeiting our long-terms goals. "This is temporary," it whispers. "This is just for today. Don't worry; you are still going to become perfect. Eat, drink, and be merry now, and you will do *teshuvah* (repent) tomorrow." And then tomorrow comes and that force distracts us for one more day, and then another. Before long, we may find ourselves reminiscing about a glorious past that wasn't, as many people do, because the painful reality is too hard to face. All this damage is wrought by what? By the "other force," also known as the *yetzer hara*.

But *"Hashem Elokeinu Hashem Echad"* means that there is no other force. The drive called *yetzer hara* — the one that will eventually cause us to regret all the time we wasted, all the years we spent vacationing from our long-terms goals — is not a messenger from some external force. Who, then, is responsible for the *yetzer hara*?

❧ Unmasking the Yetzer Hara

The answer — perhaps shockingly — is Hashem. Why would Hashem inject such a seductive force inside of us?

As we have seen, the purpose of Creation is for humanity to earn the eternal pleasure of basking in Hashem's Glory. Hashem gave us a *yetzer hara* to challenge us and make us struggle so that we can truly *enjoy* that pleasure.

> *As Succos was approaching one year, the people of Berditchev were dismayed to find that no one had managed to obtain a kosher esrog to use for the festival.*
>
> *One day a visitor came to town, and mentioned to someone that he had a kosher esrog. The townspeople tried to convince him to sell them the esrog, but he flatly refused. Then they begged him to stay there for Succos so they could use his esrog, but he insisted that he had to travel home. They offered to pay him, but he wouldn't hear of it.*
>
> *They ran to their Rebbe, Reb Levi Yitzchak, and begged him to convince the man to stay in Berditchev for Succos. Reb Levi Yitzchak asked the man whether there was anything that could get him to stay in Berditchev. "Certainly," the man responded. "If the Rebbe promises me that I will sit next to him in Olam Haba (World to Come), I will stay here for Succos and allow everyone to use my esrog."*

The Rebbe agreed, and the man sent a telegram to his family to let them know that he would not make it home for Succos.

On the first night of Succos, the man went to pray in the main shul in Berditchev, and then waited, as was customary, for someone to invite him home for the Yom Tov meal. But no invitation was forthcoming. One after another, the people filed out of shul, and he remained standing there alone.

He felt slightly embarrassed, but he had no choice but to start knocking on doors to request an invitation. He went from one house to the next, but he was refused entry into each home. He realized that something was amiss. He finally asked one of the homeowners, "Why doesn't anyone want me as a guest?"

"The Rebbe instructed us not to allow you to eat with us," he responded.

The man ran to ask the Rebbe whether he could eat with him. "No." the Rebbe answered.

"What have I done wrong? Why doesn't the Rebbe allow me to fulfill the mitzvah of eating and sleeping in a succah?"

"Because you requested something that is beyond your reach," said Reb Levi Yitzchak. "If you relinquish your right to sit next to me in the World to Come, I will allow you to eat and sleep in my succah."

The man thought about it, and decided that it would be wrong to forgo the obligation to eat in the succah in order to merit sitting next to the Rebbe in Olam Haba. He agreed to relinquish his right to the privilege, and was graciously welcomed into the Rebbe's succah.

Once he had settled and started eating, the Rebbe said, "Now I can grant you your request, and you will indeed sit next to me in the World to Come.

*"When you first made the request," the Rebbe explained, "I had no choice but to grant it, because I wanted to have an esrog. But I knew that you would not **enjoy** sitting next to me, because you weren't worthy of that level. You would have been ashamed to be the lowliest person in that lofty place.*

"Now that that you have uplifted yourself by showing that a mitzvah is so valuable to you that you are willing to forgo your request, you will enjoy sitting next to me in Olam Haba."

If Hashem would allow us to bask in His Presence without earning it, we would not be able to enjoy it. We would hang our heads in shame rather than take pleasure in it. Hashem placed us into this world and gave us a *yetzer hara* so that we can *earn* our eternal reward by prevailing over him. As we withstand the ever-increasing challenges of the *yetzer hara*, we draw closer to Hashem, and develop the ability to enjoy the ultimate pleasure of basking in His Presence in the World to Come.

Our sole purpose for existence in this world, then, is to come close to Hashem. The *yetzer hara's* sole purpose for existence is *not* to distract us from serving Hashem, but to help us grow. His entire existence is one of illusion. His role is that of a coach, who pushes an athlete to the extreme to help him attain success. When he says, "Sin," he really means, "Let me see you withstand my challenge and become great."

The *yetzer hara* may seem like a nuisance, but he sells the tickets to eternal pleasure. You cannot grow without him. You cannot perfect yourself without being challenged by increasingly difficult circumstances.

More importantly, he helps you enjoy your time here on earth. Without him life would be empty and meaningless. The more you feel the challenge and are able to prevail, the better you feel about yourself.

✒️ Bearing Down for the Battle

But what do you do when you are fighting a tight, painful battle with the *yetzer hara* and it seems that your chances for success are slim? What do you do when you reach a point when you are ready to say, "I know that this is wrong but I really need to do it"?

The Talmud (*Berachos* 5a) prescribes a course of treatment. "One should pit his *yetzer tov* against his *yetzer hara*. If that does not work, he should study Torah. If that fails, he should read *Krias Shema*. And if that also fails, he should remind himself about the day of death.

In light of what we have learned about *Yichud Hashem,* we can explain the depth of this process.

The first step in dealing with the *yetzer hara* is to pit the *yetzer tov* against him. When you feel the pain of the battle, step back and laugh. Remind yourself that the *yetzer hara* is an illusion, and that he really wants you to prevail just as the *yetzer tov* does. Remember that true satisfaction comes from overcoming the urge to sin, not from sinning.

The next step is Torah study, which helps you focus on your long-term goals and will remind you that you may forfeit those goals if you give in to the *yetzer hara*'s demands.

If Torah study does not help, read *Krias Shema*. While reciting the words, *"Hashem Echad,"* remind yourself that the *yetzer hara* is a messenger of Hashem, and that he really wants you to succeed in passing his tests.

Finally, if all else fails, remind yourself of the day you are going to die. Think about what you want to be remembered for, and what you must do if you want to be remembered for it.

❧ The Procrastination Technique

The Talmud (*Succah* 52a) states that in the End of Days, Hashem will remove the *yetzer hara* from within us, and the wicked are going to cry and say, "It looks like a strand of hair. Why couldn't we withstand the challenge?" A significant portion of the eternal suffering will be the feeling of having failed against a frail adversary that could easily have been defeated.

When we are involved in a tight battle with the *yetzer hara*, however, he does not seem to be a flimsy hair. He seems to be an unbeatable opponent. What does this passage mean?

Successful parents know that the best approach to dealing with children in the midst of a tantrum is to distract them. A child who insists on having his way will forget all about it if you distract him for an hour or two. The same approach works for the *yetzer hara*. When he tells you, "You *must* sin. You absolutely need it" — stall. The Talmud states (*Kiddushin* 30b), "A person's *yetzer hara* is renewed each day." Why must it be renewed? Because when something is real, it can be constant. It can carry from one day to the next. The *yetzer hara* is an illusion, and is controlled by moods. He cannot keep up his act for long, because as soon as your mood changes, the urge will dissipate. If you procrastinate for an hour or two, you will find that you are no longer tempted to sin.

It is the changeable nature of the *yetzer hara* that the Talmud describes as being flimsy. The sinful urge that seems so difficult to ignore blows in with the wind, and can just as easily be blown away, if you identify it for what it is: an illusion created to help you grow.

A final point: the *yetzer hara* is cunning. When tempted to engage in any form of pleasure that provides temporary happiness or pleasure — even if the urge seems to be coming from a proper source — be suspicious. If the pleasure is one that does not conflict with your long-terms goals, if it simply allows you to maintain your sanity in a world full of enticement, fine. Hashem placed such pleasures into the system and provided us with the parameters in which to enjoy them. But if you can't control yourself, if you find yourself addicted to this world, then you are no longer on your way to eternal pleasure; you are on your way to eternal disappointment.

II: Finding the Common Purpose

As we travel through life, certain circumstances seem to be loaded with opportunities for growth, while others seem to slow down our spiritual advancement. To one who has mastered *Yichud Hashem, every* situation contains some opportunity for growth and spiritual perfection, because they are all sent by the One Hashem Who wants us to perfect ourselves. Let us look at some examples:

• Death

The Talmud (*Berachos* 61b) states that while Rabbi Akiva was being tortured to death by the Romans, he recited *Shema Yisrael.* His students asked, "Rebbi, this far?"

"All my days," he responded, "I wondered when I would be able to fulfill the verse, *'You shall love Hashem … with all your soul,'* which means even if He takes your soul. Now that I have the opportunity to fulfill it, should I not do so?"

This passage is the source for all martyrs — in fact, all Jews — striving to die with *Shema Yisrael* on their lips. We are also taught that one of the greatest achievements is to die *al kiddush Hashem* (for the sanctification of God's Name).

Upon further examination, however, the concept of being happy to die seems to be the opposite of our worldview. Jews are happy here in this world, where we can grow and become closer to Hashem. When we die, the growth process ends, and our reward is limited to the level that we have attained here on earth.

Shortly before the Gaon of Vilna's passing, he gathered his tzitzis in his hands and began to cry. "Why are you crying?" his students asked.

"Here on earth," he responded, "we have unlimited opportunity for growth. For the minimal task of placing a four-cornered garment with tzitzis upon ourselves each morning, we will be rewarded immeasurably for having fulfilled mitzvos every second of the day. I am about to depart for a world where I will no longer be rewarded for my actions."

Considering that death puts an end to all opportunity for growth and perfection, why was Rabbi Akiva happy to die? And why did he choose that moment to recite *Shema*?

It seems that Rabbi Akiva's students were bothered by this very question. "We realize that the daily challenges that try to block our growth are from Hashem," they said. "But does it go this far? Death, which puts an end to growth, does not seem to dovetail with the rest of our value system. Why are you reciting *Shema* and attributing this challenge to Hashem?"

Rabbi Akiva explained that while death ends the process of growth and perfection, it actually presents the greatest opportunity to fulfill the singular purpose of Creation. The ultimate sign of a spiritually perfected person is his ability to say to Hashem, "I want to continue growing, but if Your will is that I die, I am willing to sacrifice the growth process for You." That sacrifice brings about the ultimate closeness to Hashem.

Rushka (Grizhak) Kurz was 14 when she was taken to Auschwitz. Within her first two few weeks of arrival, her best friend had passed away, and two new friends with whom she shared her barracks also died in their sleep. "That day I went to work with a heavy heart," she told her granddaughter some 50 years later. "I felt so alone and so sad. How much longer could I continue? In the evening, after a long and torturous day, I returned with all the other girls and women in our bloc. There was no preparation for bed like we had at home. There was no putting on fresh, clean pajamas or washing up and brushing teeth. Nothing like that.

There was no kiss from Mama or bedtime story from Tatty. I didn't allow myself the luxury of remembering all that, but as I climbed onto the bunk in my torn old clothing, there was one thing I never forgot. I covered my eyes and said, 'Shema Yisrael, Hashem Elokeinu, Hashem Echad,' the same way I had done back home before the war. I finished off the prayer quietly and was about to drop off in exhaustion when I heard one of the women in the lower bunk ask me, 'Why do you bother? Do your really think someone hears you?'

"She wasn't being mean or cynical — at least I didn't think so at the time. I answered her simply, the best way I could: 'This is what my mother taught me to do and this is what I have always done. I just feel it is the right thing to do. Why should I stop now — especially now, when I need it most.' "

• Obstacles to Growth

People often remark, "I could not learn today because I caught the flu." "I had planned to daven *Minchah* with a *minyan*, but my child got sick and I had to take him to the doctor." "I wanted to come on time to *Daf Yomi*, but my car wouldn't start." Such statements are usually accompanied with thoughts of, "*What a shame; I wanted to serve Hashem, but the circumstances of my life prevented me from doing so.*"

When viewed through the lenses of *Yichud Hashem*, such thoughts are ridiculous. If you think that there are forces of opposition preventing you from growing, then you lack awareness of the Oneness of Hashem. There are no forces of opposition. Colds, sick children, and car trouble come from Hashem, and they were created to bring you closer to Him no less than your *siddur* and your *gemara*. Certain levels of perfection can be attained by davening and studying Torah, and others can be attained only when you are in bed with the flu or in the waiting room of a doctor's office with your child. There are aspects of your personality that will be refined when you learn how to deal with the frustration of a car that will not start. All these obstacles are from Hashem, and they are meant to help you grow, not get in the way of your growth. If you identify them as struggles that you must overcome, they will help you attain perfection so that you can enjoy your eternal reward.

Furthermore, although we can't compare car trouble to death, they do share an underlying principle. Just as dying *al kiddush Hashem* means sacrificing the entire growth process, so too, dealing with the various obstacles that crop up may require us to sacrifice the growth process for a day, or a week, or for as long as Hashem wants us to. However, *Yichud Hashem* should provide the confidence of knowing that those obstacles also bring us closer to Hashem, because every circumstance in life is meant to bring us closer to Him.

✌❧ Planning: Allow for Change

Many *mussar* works — *Mesillas Yesharim* in particular — mention the need to set goals and track our progress in reaching them on a regular basis. Indeed, it is doubtful that one can grow spiritually without setting goals and making proper plans to achieve them. We must be aware, however, that we are not in control of our lives. We may find that our efforts are being hampered from time to time, or we may find that our plans are entirely impossible to implement. If we do not master *Yichud Hashem*, we will become frustrated when we are unable to reach our goals, and we may well blame the obstacles on external forces. Living with *Yichud Hashem* allows us to be at peace when our efforts are ruined, because we accept each obstacle as a challenge, as a message from Hashem. We are secure in the knowledge that our efforts are not in vain; each step of the way is guided by Hashem, Who wants us to succeed and grow. We know that the only true setbacks are those caused by failure to overcome the challenges or failure to read the messages Hashem is sending.

✑ Fit Everything — and Everyone — Into Your Plans

Part of *Yichud Hashem*, then, is to make sure that your plans are not too clearly defined. If you plan to learn from exactly 9 to 10, you will become upset when your plans are disturbed — whether by the weather, your health, your family obligations, or your friends. Make your plans flexible enough to adjust to all factors in your life. When you set a milestone, realize that you may have to adjust it. *Yichud Hashem* means that Hashem communicates with you constantly, and He may redirect you by using the infinite methods at His disposal to foil your plans. Don't allow your plans to become so sacred that you cannot adjust them, and you feel like a failure if everything does not go according to plan. Don't come before Hashem and say, "Here are my plans, this is where I am going, and this is the date that I plan to get there — please help me." Realize that this is *His* world, that all the obstacles come from *Him*, and be ready to adjust your plans accordingly.

The Mishnah (*Sanhedrin* 37a) states that every one of us should think, "*Bishvili nivra haolam* — the world was created for me." Superficially understood, this seems to be extremely self-centered. In the context of *Yichud Hashem*, however, we realize that this is actually a challenge. It is not the *world* that was created for you, but the *happenings* in the world around you that were created for you. The world is your challenge. Each man, woman, and child in your life was sent by Hashem at a time that He felt you needed him or her for your growth. Some can help you become great; others can cause you to stumble if you do not withstand the challenges they present. Sometimes He wants you to learn from a person, other times He wants you to help him. And there are times when a person was sent to provide an example of what you should or should *not* aspire to be. The same is true for every experience in your life. Nothing happens coincidentally. Each situation is sent by Hashem to help you attain perfection.

We often feel as though our lives are being pulled in different directions. We feel, for instance, that we should spend much of our time studying Torah, but we also realize the value of being involved in *chessed* (acts of kindness), *kiruv* (outreach), community initiatives, and many other worthy pursuits. We realize that we should also be spending time with our children. Sometimes we feel that we must sacrifice some of the time we designate for Torah study for other pursuits.

Yichud Hashem means that you are not *sacrificing* one spiritual pursuit for another. Torah study, *chessed*, *kiruv*, and child-rearing all have one purpose: to cause you to come closer to perfection, to come closer to Hashem. They do not compete for your time, rather they fit together to form the puzzle of spiritual perfection. There are times when you must focus on Torah study so that you can know Hashem and learn to emulate Him, and there are times when you must emulate Him in practice. The key is to find the correct balance and not let one mitzvah crowd out another.

And it is important to remember that the situation itself was also created by Hashem. He wants you to struggle with the question. It would be so much easier if the Torah would tell us exactly how much time to spend studying, how much time to spend helping others, and exactly how long *Shemoneh Esrei* should take. But the road to perfection is full of difficulty and struggle, necessarily so. Learning to judge your own capabilities, learning to evaluate all the responsibilities in your life and invest the proper amount of time into each are part of the growth process. Hashem wants you to struggle with the dilemma, to make decisions and follow through in action, but to be willing to adjust and change your plans when He sends you new challenges and messages.

ᴥᓮ All One Purpose

Until now, we have been discussing the need to find the correct balance between different types of spiritual pursuits. *Yichud Hashem* goes much further.

When we develop our plans for life, we tend to "compartmentalize." We have a spiritual compartment that contains Torah study, prayer, *chessed*, and all other aspects of service of Hashem, and a compartment for "regular" life activities: eating, sleeping, working, vacationing, etc. We feel as if we lead "double lives," splitting our time between holy activities that are part of our *avodas Hashem*, and other activities that seem materialistic and detached from Hashem.

Yichud Hashem teaches that no such separation exists. The very same Hashem Who commands us to study Torah and daven also wants us to sleep and eat so that we should have strength to serve Him, and He wants us to support our families. All activities — ones that feel holy and ones that seem mundane — are part of the service of Hashem, as long as we engage in them in the correct parameters and with the correct intentions.

> When the milkman of Bayit Vegan passed away, Rabbi Eliyahu (Elyah) Lopian instructed yeshivah students to attend his funeral. When asked what was so special about him, Rav Elyah explained that he had once asked the elderly milkman why he did not retire. "You are an old man. Why do you continue to rise at 3 a.m. and ride your donkey out to the farm to purchase the milk and then make dozens of trips up and down the steps of the buildings with heavy milk canisters on your shoulders?"
>
> "I do it," the milkman had explained, "so that mothers will have milk to give to their children."
>
> "This man lived for mitzvos," Rav Elyah continued. "He did not work for his own livelihood, but to provide others with a much-needed staple. It is appropriate that we honor such a devout servant of Hashem by attending his funeral."
>
> A similar incident occurred when Rav Elyah needed medication late one evening. He found out that one pharmacy stayed open until midnight, and traveled there to pick up the medicine. "Thank you so much," he said to the pharmacist. "It is so kind of you to stay open late to provide medicine for those in need."

"Kind?" the pharmacist said. "I'm not doing anyone a favor. By law, each pharmacy must stay open one night a week, and tonight is my night. I'm here because I am required to be here."

"What a shame," Rav Elyah responded. "If only you would have stayed open with the intention of helping people, you would be rewarded immeasurably for all eternity for providing this vital service. Instead, all you have to show for your efforts is some money."

We must have *Yichud Hashem* in mind constantly, because we are challenged by Hashem every second of the day. Sometimes the challenge is to study Torah, and sometimes the challenge is to go to sleep. But don't go to sleep merely because you enjoy your bed. Realize that Hashem *wants* you to rest so that you can serve Him better in your waking hours. Go to sleep for the same reason that you learn: to serve Hashem and come close to Him. If you have an errand to tend to, don't view it as a nuisance. Realize that Hashem sent it your way, and He wants you to grow from it.

On a larger scale, when planning your life, your year, or even your day, place all your activities into an equation. Realize that One Hashem has given you the responsibilities of supporting a family, of helping those around you, and of coming to know Him through His Torah. Don't balance two sides of an equation, weighing the spiritual against the material. All the factors should be on one side of the equation, and the result should be the sum total of your *avodas Hashem*, for everything you do and all that you acquire can help you along the road to spiritual perfection.

◆§ No Fear

The middle blessing of *Shemoneh Esrei* of Shabbos *Minchah* begins with the words: אַתָּה אֶחָד וְשִׁמְךָ אֶחָד, *You are One and Your Name is One,* וּמִי כְּעַמְּךָ יִשְׂרָאֵל גּוֹי אֶחָד בָּאָרֶץ, *and who is like Your nation, Israel, one nation in the land.* This blessing is a description of the End of Days, when everyone will realize that Hashem is One.

Then we will know Hashem through only one Name;[4] we will no longer perceive different systems controlling the world. Klal Yisrael will be united, serving Hashem in perfect harmony.

The paragraph ends with a description of the frame of mind we will experience in those days: מְנוּחַת שָׁלוֹם וְשַׁלְוָה וְהַשְׁקֵט, *total peace of mind; pure tranquility*. When we fail to recognize the unity of purpose in the world, we are confused and broken. We feel great one day because we feel that we were able to devote ourselves to spiritual pursuits, and dejected the next day, when we feel that we have not grown. We constantly change our mind and our mood, and we don't feel comfortable with ourselves. When we will have absolute unity of purpose, we will feel at peace with ourselves.

But then there is one more word in the blessing: וָבֶטַח — *security.* There will no longer be any fear. While the ultimate security will be felt only in the End of Days, the message here is clear: *Yichud Hashem* should bring us security and make us fearless. Why?

When you are firmly convinced that there is unity in purpose — when you firmly believe that all of our challenges come from Hashem and will help us grow — what is there to fear? That Hashem will send a surprise challenge that you were not expecting? That's no reason to be fearful! Hashem sends only the challenges that are best for you and that you are capable of conquering. The worst thing that can happen is that Hashem will send you a message that you must take a different path to perfection. It might mean that you will have to endure difficulty; it might come with a certain amount of pain — but it will be for your good, and you will be capable of passing the test.

The Jewish population of Europe was going through particularly difficult times at some point during the late 1800's. Aside from the constant threat of pogroms and exile, danger lurked in

---

4. The Names of Hashem represent different attributes of Divine control of the world. For instance, the Tetragrammaton (*Yud-Hei-Vav-Hei*) represents Divine Mercy, and *Elokim* represents Justice.

the form of diseases that ran rampant through shtetls, striking down hundreds of people. One weekday morning, the Rebbe of a Chassidic community sent a message to his townspeople: they should all be in the shul at 7 p.m., and he would address them.

What was the Rebbe going to talk about? What important message would he share with them?

That evening, the streets were silent, as everyone sat in the shul. The Rebbe walked in, strode purposefully to the Aron Kodesh, opened it, and put his hand on one of the Sifrei Torah.

"My dear Chassidim," he said. "I beg of each of you, if there is ever a moment in your lives when you feel that you are not being tested, when you feel that life is flowing smoothly and seamlessly, stop whatever you are doing and run to the shul. Open the Aron Kodesh, place your head between the Sifrei Torah, and cry your heart out. When you finish, raise your eyes to the Heavens and say, 'Hashem, why did You decide to let my life flow without any challenge? Did You lose confidence in me?' "

To a person who has internalized the message of *Yichud Hashem*, challenges are not an unfortunate fact of life, but a sign of Hashem's trust and confidence in his ability to succeed.

❧ Shema as a Barometer

We raised some basic questions as we set out to learn about *Yichud Hashem*. We are now equipped with the knowledge necessary to answer those questions.

First, we wondered why there would be a commandment to recite *Shema Yisrael* twice daily if we must focus on it constantly. We have learned that *Yichud Hashem* requires us to realize that we live for only one purpose: to attain spiritual perfection so that we will be able to take eternal pleasure from Hashem. We also learned that we have a coach, the *yetzer hara*, trying to help us grow by presenting us with deceptive challenges that we must overcome. The two parts to the mitzvah — the recitation morning and evening, and the constant aspect — address these two points.

With so much distraction in the busy world around us, we can easily lose sight of our goal. We can spend our lives in pursuit of pettiness and forget about the gold mine that Hashem has made available to us. When we recite *Shema* morning and evening, we start and end our day by reminding ourselves that we live only to take eternal pleasure from Hashem, and that we can receive that pleasure only if we direct *all* our actions toward that purpose. We remind ourselves that anything else we may be pursuing is meaningless, temporary, and superficial.

> *A poor man once approached a wealthy member of his community and begged him for a job. "My wife and children are starving," he said, "and if I don't start earning money soon, they might die." The rich man thought about it for a few moments, and out of pity, he decided to hire the man as his personal assistant.*
>
> *Several months later, the wealthy man had to travel away from home for a few days. He called his assistant and handed him a paper with step-by-step instructions on how to handle his home and business while he would be away. "Read the instructions each morning so that you do not forget what you must do," he said as he got into his wagon.*
>
> *Several days later, the man came home and summoned his assistant. "Did you follow my orders?" he asked.*
>
> *"Certainly," the fellow responded. "Each morning I came to your home, sat down on the couch, and read the paper with your instructions from beginning to end. When I finished, I read it again, and again, until it was time to go home."*
>
> *"Fool!" the wealthy man thundered. "Do you think that I wanted you to read that paper for your leisure? I wanted you to follow the instructions, not just read them."*

The Chofetz Chaim offered this story as a parable for our sojourn here on earth. Hashem sends us into this world on a mission, and provides us with instructions. He commands us to read a summary of those instructions twice daily to remind ourselves that we are here for a reason. Unfortunate are those who read Shema simply to fulfill the commandment of reciting it, without giving a moment's notice to the instructions therein.

The recitation of *Shema* can also serve as a barometer — two times in the day when you can pinpoint the specific challenges that the *yetzer hara* is forcing upon you that day. Before reciting *Shema*, think about the areas in life in which your belief in the Oneness of Hashem is being challenged. Identify the situations in which you do not see the *yetzer hara* as a coach or as an illusion, but as a real force to be dealt with. Once you locate those issues, recite, "*Hashem Elokeinu Hashem Echad*," with intensity, and think, "I know the truth. I know that the *yetzer hara* is an illusion. I know Who sent him and why He sent him, and I am ready to withstand his challenges." Turn the saying of *Shema Yisrael* into mile markers in your fight against the *yetzer hara*.

Yichud Hashem is also a constant mitzvah, however it is not enough to think about it twice a day; one must be on guard at all times. Whenever you feel a force from within that is trying to get you to do something that you know is wrong, remember that it is an illusion. Remember that it is not telling you to sin; it is telling you, "Let's see you overcome this difficult challenge that I have created for you." And remember that it is not from some external force, but from Hashem Himself, Who wants you to attain perfection so that you can deserve to bask in His Presence eternally.

Finally, we asked what *Yichud Hashem* adds to our service of Hashem once we have mastered the mitzvos of *Emunah* and *Lo Yihiyeh*.

In *Emunah* we learned that God is present and that He created the world for a purpose. In *Lo Yihiyeh* we learned that no other forces have any power of their own. Now we take those mitzvos to a higher plane by recognizing that there are no external forces; everything was created by Hashem to enable us to take part in His Divine — and unified — purpose.

MITZVAH REVIEW

Constant
Mitzvah

3

מצוה
תמידית

יִחוּד ה' — HASHEM'S ONENESS

The Constant Mitzvah of *Yichud Hashem* requires us to be aware that all that exists in this world is Hashem. In practical terms, this requires us to realize that no external forces have true existence. Everything that we perceive, whether it seems to be spiritual and related to growth, or material and unrelated to growth, is a manifestation of Godliness. Even the *yetzer hara*, which seems to block our way to growth, has been "programmed" into our psyche by Hashem, to foster our efforts toward greatness by presenting us with challenges that we must overcome. We grow from persevering in the struggle.

Furthermore, every event, person, and obligation in life was set in place by Hashem, Who orchestrates circumstances in such a way that the people around you can help you grow. Problems as diverse as car trouble, unexpected doctor visits, and even death, are as much a part of the growth process as Torah study and mitzvah observance.

Practical Applications of Yichud Hashem

(1) Identify the *yetzer hara* as a messenger from Hashem that challenges you and helps you grow. When you

hear the *yetzer hara* say, "Sin," interpret it to mean, "Don't sin; overcome my temptation so that you can become great."

(2) When you feel the urge to sin, procrastinate. An urge that now seems impossible to withstand will generally subside with time.

(3) Hashem wants us to enjoy His world within the correct parameters. Be careful, however, to determine which pleasures will help you grow and perfect yourself, and which are temporal and will leave you feeling empty.

(4) View all the people and obligations in your life as *part* of your *avodas Hashem*, not as obstacles to it.

(5) Realize that all circumstances in life — even those that seem to obstruct your growth — are orchestrated by Hashem to enable you to perfect yourself. Consider circumstances that prevent you from studying Torah or observing mitzvos as opportunities to perfect yourself in other areas, not as obstructions to growth. Then, every moment of life can become part of your quest for spiritual perfection.

(6) Use recitations of *Shema* as mile-markers in realizing the unity of purpose in your life's mission. Before reciting *Shema*, pause for a few moments and pinpoint areas in which the *yetzer hara* has duped you into believing that there is some other force controlling your life. Then, recite *Shema* with the intention of erasing that mistaken philosophy from your mind.

Additive Effect of Yichud Hashem

*E**munah* is an awareness of Hashem's existence and His purpose for the world. *Lo Yihiyeh* adds the awareness that no other force has any power, and that no purpose other than Hashem's is worth pursuing.

Yichud Hashem takes those awarenesses to a new level by making us realize that nothing exists other than Hashem. *Yichud Hashem* also teaches that there is unity in purpose, and that *all* circumstances in life are meant to help us grow and participate in that purpose

מִצְוָה תְּמִידִי
CONSTANT MITZVAH
4

אַהֲבַת ה'
Loving Hashem

לזכר נשמות

ישראל יהודה ב"ר יוסף דוב ז"ל רעבענוואָרצעל
ורעיתו **יעקפקע יהודית בת ר' אברהם ע"ה**

שמואל צבי ב"ר משה ז"ל הרמן
ורעיתו **שיינדל יפה בת ר' יצחק ע"ה**

נתרם על ידי
אברהם (פיטר) ושרה נוחה (דבי) רעבענוואָרצעל
משה ויחידה ברכה האס
משה דוב ויכט מינדל רעבענוואָרצעל
אליהו מאיר אלחנן ודינה אסתר גבאי
ומשפחתם

מִצְוַת אַהֲבַת ה'
The mitzvah to love Hashem

שֶׁנִּצְטַוֵּינוּ לֶאֱהוֹב אֶת הַמָּקוֹם בָּרוּךְ הוּא, שֶׁנֶּאֱמַר [דברים ו, ה]
"וְאָהַבְתָּ אֵת ה' אֱלֹהֶיךָ". וְעִנְיַן הַמִּצְוָה שֶׁנַּחְשׁוֹב וְנִתְבּוֹנֵן בְּפִקּוּדָיו
וּפְעוּלוֹתָיו עַד שֶׁנַּשִּׂיגֵהוּ כְּפִי יְכָלְתֵּנוּ, וְנִתְעַנֵּג בְּהַשָּׂגָתוֹ בְּתַכְלִית
הָעוֹנֶג, וְזֹאת הִיא הָאַהֲבָה הַמְחוּיֶּיבֶת. וּלְשׁוֹן סִפְרֵי [כאן], לְפִי
שֶׁנֶּאֱמַר"וְאָהַבְתָּ" אֵינִי יוֹדֵעַ כֵּיצַד אוֹהֵב אָדָם הַמָּקוֹם, תַּלְמוּד
לוֹמַר "וְהָיוּ הַדְּבָרִים הָאֵלֶּה אֲשֶׁר אָנֹכִי מְצַוְּךָ הַיּוֹם עַל לְבָבֶךָ",
שֶׁמִּתּוֹךְ כָּךְ אַתָּה מַכִּיר אֶת מִי שֶׁאָמַר וְהָיָה הָעוֹלָם. כְּלוֹמַר, שֶׁעִם
הִתְבּוֹנְנוּת בַּתּוֹרָה תִּתְיַשֵּׁב הָאַהֲבָה בַּלֵּב בְּהֶכְרֵחַ. וְאָמְרוּ זִכְרוֹנָם
לִבְרָכָה [שם] שֶׁזֹּאת הָאַהֲבָה תְּחַיֵּיב הָאָדָם לְעוֹרֵר בְּנֵי אָדָם
בְּאַהֲבָתוֹ לְעָבְדוֹ, כְּמוֹ שֶׁמָּצִינוּ בְּאַבְרָהָם.

We are commanded to love Hashem, blessed is He, as the verse states, "You shall love Hashem, your God" (*Devarim* 6:5). The idea of this mitzvah is that we should think about and contemplate [Hashem's] commandments and creations, so that we appreciate them to the best of our ability, and take extreme pleasure in that understanding. This (pleasure) is the love of Hashem that we are obligated to have. In the words of *Sifri* (to this verse):

"From the words 'You shall love,' one does not know *how* to come to love Hashem. Therefore, the Torah continues, 'And these words that I command you today shall be on your heart' (ibid. verse 6). It is through this (i.e., having the words of the Torah on one's heart) that you can recognize the One Who proclaimed and the world came to be."

This is to say that if you think into the Torah, the love of Hashem will inevitably become ingrained in your heart.

Our sages said (ibid.) that this love of Hashem will cause a person to inspire others to love Hashem and serve Him, as was the case with Avraham Avinu.

(*Chinuch, Mitzvah* 418)

I: Building Love

The source for the mitzvah to love God is the verse: וְאָהַבְתָּ אֵת ה' אֱלֹקֶיךָ בְּכָל לְבָבְךָ וּבְכָל נַפְשְׁךָ וּבְכָל מְאֹדֶךָ, *You shall love Hashem, your God, with all your heart, with all your soul, and with all your resources (Devarim 6:5).*

⇜ A New Set of Mitzvos

Before examining the mitzvah itself, we must note that we are now beginning a new set of mitzvos. Whereas the first three mitzvos — *Emunah, Lo Yihiyeh,* and *Yichud Hashem* — focused on the philosophical aspect of what Hashem is, beginning with *Ahavas Hashem* we work on developing a relationship with the God that we defined in the previous mitzvos. The mitzvah of *Ahavas Hashem*, for instance, requires us to move beyond the realization that there is a God, and develop an emotional attachment to Him.

The first question that comes to mind regarding *Ahavas Hashem* is one that is asked regarding several other mitzvos as well. Love is not an action, it is an emotion. We can understand how the Torah can hold us responsible for mitzvos that require action or even complex thought processes such as those necessary for the first three constant mitzvos. Emotions, however, are problematic. Many factors trigger emotions, and many others suppress them. We often find ourselves struggling to understand why certain circumstances irritate us while we handle others with equanimity. How, then, can the Torah dictate what our emotions should be? How can we develop love for God? Certainly we cannot fake it. God knows the truth!

There is another significant difficulty with this mitzvah. We know how to love finite beings — those we can see, communicate with, and get responses from; we can identify with them and interact with them. How can we develop love for an Infinite Being — especially since we are not supposed to visualize mental images of Him?

۵§ Defining Love

In order to define love of God, we must first develop a general definition for the term "love."

> There was once a person who became famous for his love of fish. One day a man came to visit him, expecting to find him in a home that resembled an aquatic zoo. But instead of observing fish carefully tagged and cared for swimming in beautifully decorated aquariums, the visitor saw the fish-lover take a fish, clobber it over the head, cut out its intestines, roast it, and serve it to a group of friends. The visitor was terribly disappointed. "You don't love fish," he told the professed fish-lover. "You love yourself, and you satisfy your desire to please yourself by eating fish."[1]

───────────

1. This parable appears in various forms in many *mussar* works (see *Lev Eliyahu, Parashas Vayeitzei*).

When someone says that he loves someone or something, quite often his true intention is that he loves *himself* and that the subject or object of his love helps satisfy his desire to please himself. True love, however, is not to take from someone else, but to be so taken by that person that you want to please him and enjoy his presence as much as possible. *Pirkei Avos* compares selfish love to that of Amnon for Tamar, and true love to that of David and Yonasan. Amnon's love for Tamar was based purely on his desire for personal gratification. Once that was satisfied, the love was gone. David and Yonasan, on the other hand, had every reason to be enemies, because they could have considered themselves as rivals competing for the right to become king. Because there was no element of selfishness in their love for each other, their friendship was pure and enduring. It transcended all obstacles.

◆§ Developing Love for God

Now that we have defined love, let us return to our questions. How do we create an emotion and maintain it every second of our lives, and especially for a Being that is abstract?

From the *Rishonim*'s approach to *Ahavas Hashem* it is obvious that there is no way to *create* emotions. Rather than focus on building emotions, they recommend specific actions that will cause us to love Hashem:

(1) Studying Nature

In discussing the path toward both love and fear of God, Rambam (*Hilchos Yesodei HaTorah* 2:2) writes:

> When a person focuses on Hashem's wondrous acts and creations and recognizes His infinite and unmatched wisdom, he will immediately be filled with love and praise for Hashem, and he will desire to know Him, as King David said: צָמְאָה נַפְשִׁי לֵאלֹקִים לְקֵל חָי, *My soul thirsts for God, for the living God* (*Tehillim* 42:3).

Indeed, it may be nearly impossible to develop emotions for an Infinite Being to Whom we cannot relate. But Rambam teaches that when we think about the greatness and wisdom of Hashem, we will be overcome by a passionate desire to come closer to Him. In other words, we will want to spend all of our time in His presence, or in Ramchal's words (*Mesillas Yesharim* 1), we will want to remove all the barriers that separate us from Him.

Rambam follows his description of the route to *Ahavas Hashem* by delving into the secrets of nature, most of which are beyond us, with the intention of "opening the gates of love of Hashem to those who will understand." In truth, however, we need not explore the *secrets* of nature; the basic elements are enough to fill a thinking person with wonder and love for the Creator.

> *Rabbi Elazer Menachem Man Shach would often marvel at the beauty of Creation. He would point out how perfectly geometric an orange is, and how palatable Hashem made it for us to eat.*
>
> *Rabbi Avigdor Miller was known for his command of biology. But beyond his ability to describe the wisdom that is evident in each component of nature, he once demonstrated the importance of associating that wisdom with Hashem.*
>
> *Rabbi Miller's grandson once walked into his grandfather's house and found him with his head immersed in the kitchen sink, which he had filled with water. "I overheard someone complaining about the smog and pollution that fills the air of New York," Rabbi Miller explained to his startled visitor when he came up for air. "I wanted to make sure that his comment did not affect my appreciation of the air Hashem provides for us. When you have your head underwater long enough and realize what it means not to have any air, you appreciate what Hashem provides — whether humans pollute it or not."*

(2) Studying Torah

Chinuch writes:

> [To love Hashem] is to study His commandments and His deeds until we gain an understanding of them — according

to our ability — and to *take extreme pleasure in that understanding*. This is the love that is required of us, as *Sifri* (*Devarim* 6:5) states: "If it would state only: [וְאָהַבְתָּ [אֵת ה' אֱלֹקֶיךָ, *You shall love [Hashem, your God]*, I would not know how one comes to love Hashem. Therefore, the Torah continues: וְהָיוּ הַדְּבָרִים הָאֵלֶּה אֲשֶׁר אָנֹכִי מְצַוְּךָ הַיּוֹם עַל לְבָבֶךָ, *And these matters that I command you today shall be upon your heart ...*"

That is, if you delve into Torah study, love of Hashem will — most definitely — fill your heart.

(3) Mesirus Nefesh

In commenting on a verse in which Hashem pledges to show kindness to those who love Him, Ramban (*Shemos* 20:5) quotes a Midrash:

> [Those who love Me] refers to Jews who dwell in Eretz Yisrael and sacrifice their lives for the sake of mitzvah observance.

The Midrash goes on to record a hypothetical conversation with Jews who sacrificed for Hashem:

> Why are you being executed?
> Because I circumcised my son.
> Why are you being burned at the stake?
> Because I studied Torah.
> Why are you being hanged?
> Because I ate matzah.
> Why are you being whipped?
> Because I shook a *lulav* (on Succos).

According to Ramban, our love for Hashem strengthens and increases when we suffer for Him, because physical sacrifice for His sake makes us aware of a deep, burning love for Him that already exists in our subconscious mind.

≈§ Yogurt on Your Glasses

Our study of these *Rishonim* should lead us to conclude:

- That every scientist must love Hashem passionately, for the more you know about nature, the more you love Hashem.
- That anyone who studies Torah loves Hashem, and that the love for Him should increase in proportion to the amount of Torah one studies.
- That anyone who suffered for Hashem must love Him.

In reality, however, the scientific world is staffed by thousands of declared atheists. In our times, many scientists have become so captivated with the theory of evolution, which allows people to deny the existence of a Higher Being, that they refuse to allow any debate on the matter. In a landmark case, a Texas School Board was threatened by university professors that if their students were taught to question the theory of evolution, they might not be accepted into a university. And when Dr. Francis S. Collins was nominated to head the National Institutes of Health, many scientists objected to his nomination because he is a believer in God.

It seems that in the case of many scientists nowadays, not only does the study of nature fail to bring about love for Hashem — on the contrary, it causes them to deny His existence.

While not nearly so striking, the same issue exists in regard to Torah study. There are people who spend years of their lives in intensive Torah study and do not feel the love of Hashem filling their hearts.

And as far as suffering is concerned, the Holocaust — among many other tragedies that struck our nation — left millions of Jews without love for Hashem. Now, obviously, the *Rishonim* are not wrong, so how do we resolve the contradiction between their statements that these methods are guaranteed to cause us to love God and what seems to be the reality?

The answer to this question can be derived from a legend made famous by a rosh yeshivah of Telshe. A man once visited the Louvre, one of the world's premiere art museums. As he walked from one painting to the next, he began to voice his disappointment in the artwork. "This is what they call beautiful?" he asked, standing next to one painting. "It looks like yogurt!" He moved on to the next masterpiece, and once again announced, "Yogurt!" When he criticized the third piece with the very same description, a man standing next to him asked, "Can I see your glasses?"

The critic removed his glasses and handed them to the fellow, who held them up to the light. "Of course all you see is yogurt," he exclaimed, "The lenses of your glasses are covered with yogurt!"

The *Rishonim's* methods for building love for Hashem are indeed foolproof — as long as the practitioner *wants* to build love for Hashem. If someone studies nature, studies Torah, or sacrifices for Hashem, and he does not feel his heart overflowing with love for Him, something must be wrong. His vision must be blocked by "yogurt." There must be some issue that is causing him to avoid Hashem. In order to feel love, one has to *want* to feel it, not seek to avoid it.

> *On April 12, 1961, Russian cosmonaut Yuri Gagarin became the first person to travel in space. Nikita Khrushchev, the Soviet premier, reported that Gagarin proved that there was no God, because he did not see Him while up in orbit.*
>
> *The utter foolishness of Khrushchev's statement is astounding. We know that God is not physical and cannot be seen. But even if Khrushchev were expecting Gagarin to see some sort of physical manifestation of God in space, the lack of such a vision proved nothing. The Vostok capsule that propelled him into space barely cleared the gravitational pull of earth, and orbited only several times before coming back to earth. Even with Khrushchev's shallow understanding of what God should be, Gagarin may have missed Him because He was beyond the capsule's altitude. It is obvious that this statement was made with little consideration by a person whose personal view clouded his judgment.*

In contrast, seven years later, American astronauts on the Apollo 8 mission were the first to broadcast pictures of earth, taken from space, on national media. Toward the end of their mission, the three crew members recited the first ten verses of Genesis, relating the story of Creation.

In July of 1969, U.S. astronauts Neil Armstrong and Buzz Aldrin became the first humans to set foot on the moon. In a broadcast shown nationwide on the night before they landed, Aldrin said, "Personally, in reflecting on the events of the past several days, a verse from Psalms comes to mind: 'When I consider the heavens, the work of Thy fingers, the moon and the stars which Thou hast ordained; what is man that Thou art mindful of him?'"

The difference between the reactions of the Russian cosmonaut and the American astronauts begs an explanation. Does the experience of traveling in outer space — or any other study of nature — cause a person to become a greater believer in God, or does it make one doubt? The answer is that it depends on the person's prior mindset. Someone who enters space with the intention of proving his atheistic belief is likely to emerge with the foolish observation made by Khrushchev. The key to growth through nature — and all other methods mentioned by the *Rishonim* — is open-mindedness. If we find ourselves unaffected by the study of nature or the study of Torah, or by suffering, then we must have yogurt on our glasses. There must be some agenda that prevents us from viewing the evidence with an open mind. What is that agenda?

Secular people may fear — subconsciously — that impartial examination of the evidence will result in positive proof of the existence of a Creator, which would mean that there must be purpose to life, and that the world is not a free-for-all. Since the existence of a Creator will require them to change their lifestyles, their study of nature is distorted by their determination to find proof for their prior beliefs. No matter how convincing the evidence is, they will always find reason to argue or ignore it.

For religious Jews, too, there is much to fear. Many of us are ready to focus on God to the extent that it does not restrict us *too much*, but we have our limits. When we find something that seems to threaten the comfort of our existence, we make sure not to focus on it too intently. And even if we do allow ourselves to study such information on an intellectual level, sometimes it is not our eyes that are being blocked, but our heart. We cannot find it within ourselves to make the emotional change that is necessary.

Success in *Ahavas Hashem* is dependent on open-mindedness. The first step to impartial investigation of nature and Torah is to recognize that the fear that prevents us from doing so is the fear of the unknown. We don't *know* that a life of closeness to Hashem will be painful and make us unhappy, but we are *afraid* that it might. That fear brings an inability to see the beauty of a life with Hashem. We get caught up in a track of circular reasoning: we are afraid that the restrictions imposed by a God-filled existence will make us unhappy, so we refrain from investigating how beautiful such a lifestyle is and how happy it will make us.

The *Rishonim*'s approach to *Ahavas Hashem* is effective, but only for those who are able to remove these obstacles. We must learn to impartially examine each piece of information we learn, and see where it leads us. We must not be afraid of seeing how beautiful life can be when we realize that we are not restricted; we should focus on what we realize is the true importance of life. We must be brave enough to embrace a life in which we don't feel any temptation to break the rules, because we are so clear about where we want to go and how we are going to get there.

☙ A Second Look

Now that our glasses are clean, we can reexamine nature, Torah, and suffering and see whether they affect us as they should.

• Nature

Let us begin with nature, the factor that Rambam (*Yesodei HaTorah* 2:2) seems to consider most likely to cause us to love Hashem. Upon viewing a previously unseen aspect of nature, we are instinctively captivated by its beauty and perfection. The challenge is to associate it with Hashem, and realize how the perfect harmony attests to the existence of a Creator. Realize that no supercomputer or super-anything could create even one aspect of nature spontaneously, let alone the countless number of magnificent creations that surround us. The most amazing innovations in science require raw materials that Hashem has provided; human science cannot manufacture anything *ex nihilo*.

When we begin to notice the wisdom, caring, and understanding that is invested into each mountain, river, houseplant, and butterfly, we will undoubtedly be awestruck by Hashem's Greatness.

We need not take field trips in order to appreciate Hashem's amazing Creation. The information that the average high-school student is taught provides enough proof of the perfection and wondrousness of nature. Furthermore, the advent of modern technology places us in a better position than ever to appreciate the astonishing wisdom of Creation. The most important components of computers are drawn from nature. Taking it one step further, the human brain that was able to create the computer certainly was not created — and cannot be recreated — by humans.

With a little bit of thought, this should lead us to the certainty of the existence of a Creator. Indeed, scientists who spend their time delving deeper and deeper into the amazing depth and orderliness of Creation should lead the world in proclaiming that there is a God.

The aforementioned Dr. Francis S. Collins was a confirmed atheist until he opened his mind to the possibility of God and the evidence for a Creator Who made what science can only study and attempt to recreate. He began to realize that it took greater faith and a considerable amount of arrogance to be an atheist and to reject any evidence to the contrary.

As leader of the Human Genome Project, Dr. Collins led a team of more than 2,000 scientists from six countries. "Together," he said, "we determined all three billion letters of the human genome, and [produced] our own DNA instruction book.

"It is hard to get your mind around how much information this is. Suppose we decided to take a little time this morning to read the letters of the human genome together, just to express our awe at God's creation. If we took turns reading, and agreed to stick with it until we were all the way through, we would be here for 31 years! And you have all that information inside each of the 100 trillion cells of your body."

It takes a lot of faith (or denial) to believe that random chance produced such order in the human body, or the order in the rest of the observable universe.

The deeper our knowledge and understanding of nature becomes, the more convinced we should be of the existence of a Creator. But additionally, when we appreciate the breathtaking perfection in Creation and link it with the Creator, we should feel a need to come close to Him and to love Him.

• Torah

A person who studies Torah superficially will not be awestruck by it — although he may find the task of understanding it quite overwhelming. If one's appreciation of *Chumash* is limited to short insights into the weekly *parashah* (Torah portion), and Talmud is a study that he finds frustrating because its relevance is not always apparent, he will not come to love Hashem by studying Torah.

When you study *Chumash*, work on finding the messages that are hidden in the seemingly insignificant details of each verse. Realize that each grammatical nuance and choice of phraseology

DAY 32

contains information. There are valuable lessons to be gleaned from the Torah's descriptions — lessons that can provide practical solutions to problems we face.

> *On the subway in New York City, the Ponevezher Rav, Rabbi Yosef Shlomo Kahaneman, noticed a group of hoodlums glancing secretly in his direction. He sensed that they were about to attack him, and he was carrying a large sum of money that he had raised for his yeshivah. Thinking quickly, he took a note out of his pocket and approached the group. Pointing to an address that was written on the paper, he asked, "Can you please tell me how I get to this address?"*
>
> *Smiling slightly at the naïveté of the elderly rabbi, the leader of the group said, "We'll do even better — we will take you there. Just get off at the next stop with us and we'll show you where it is."*
>
> *When the doors of the train opened at the next station, the Rav made a sweeping gesture toward the doors with his hand, honoring his "escorts" to exit first. After they stepped off onto the platform, the Rav readied himself as if he were about to step down. He delayed just long enough to allow the doors to begin sliding shut, and then he quickly retreated into the car, leaving the group of thugs stranded on the platform as the train pulled away with him inside it.*
>
> *Later, he told Rav Abba Grossbard that he had devised his plan based on a verse in the Torah. In Parashas Vayishlach, after Yaakov made peace with Eisav, the latter offered to travel together with him. Yaakov preferred not to have the company of his wicked brother, but did not want to upset the fragile peace agreement they had reached. "Let my lord go ahead of his servant," he told Eisav, "I will make my way at my slow pace according to the gait of the flock before me and the gait of the children, until I come to my lord at Seir" (Bereishis 33:14).*
>
> *"In truth," said the Ponevezher Rav, "Yaakov had no intention of traveling to Seir. He knew that living in close proximity to Eisav would be dangerous — both physically and spiritually. He*

avoided insulting Eisav by telling him to go ahead, and that he (Yaakov) would catch up. I learned from this verse that when a Jew must remove himself from enemies who want to harm him, he can do so by pretending to go along with them, but moving at a slower pace and leaving them waiting for him. That is what I did on the train."

Yeshivah students spend hours — even days or weeks at times — trying to understand the depth of a *sugya* (Talmudic topic). The process requires mind-numbing concentration, and an approach will often be proven wrong after much time and mental energy was invested into developing it. But the absolute certainty that there is a truly perfect approach keeps them going. They try and try until they find the correct approach, and when they do, they experience indescribable joy.

> *On a snowy, cold day in Yerushalayim, Rav Dovid Finkel decided to visit the Brisker Rav, figuring that he would have plenty of time to spend with the Rav on a day when no one else would venture out to visit him. As he reached the Brisker Rav's street, he saw a lone figure dancing in the snow. Upon drawing near he recognized the dancer as none other than Rav Shach. When he asked Rav Shach why he was dancing, the latter explained, "The Brisker Rav's explanations of Torah concepts fill me with such joy that I want to dance each time I leave his house. I usually suppress my emotions, however, because I know that passersby will consider it strange, but on a snowy day like today I was sure no one would be outside, so I allowed myself to rejoice in this manner."*
>
> *On a similar note, Rav Shach once remarked that he did not understand why people felt drawn to material pleasures. "I just finished a Torah discussion with the Brisker Rav. I cannot think of anything more pleasurable than hearing his Torah thoughts!"*

Once you begin to study Torah in depth, you will start to feel intense love for the One Who gave it to the Jewish people. And once you begin to feel that love, you will develop a craving for more and more Torah knowledge. You will yearn to find more time to study Torah so that you can increase your appreciation of the One you are in love with.

Torah study is, therefore, a clear indicator of where you stand in your efforts to build *Ahavas Hashem*. When studying ceases to be a chore and becomes a passion, you know that you have become a true *oheiv Hashem*.

• Suffering

Finally, Ramban, based on the Midrash, teaches that suffering for Hashem will cause us to love Him. The question of why we suffer is not limited to tragedies of epic proportions. Although the Midrash focuses primarily on those dying for Hashem, Ramban applies it to any form of suffering. Life is tough, and we go through much hardship. Rare is the moment when we find ourselves without some issue to struggle with. We may be willing to overlook our difficulties when we compare them to those of friends or neighbors whom we consider more unfortunate than us, but in truth, since the world was created for us and our pleasure, we should never suffer.[2] If we do, we must try to figure out why Hashem is bringing it upon us. We must take an honest look at our lives and try to interpret the messages Hashem is sending. We must determine which areas in life He wants us to repair. We must make sure that we are not ignoring our suffering simply because we feel comfortable with our spiritual standing and don't want to exert ourselves to improve it.

Suffering can therefore bring us closer to Hashem, but only if we crave that closeness. If we are afraid to come closer to Him because we think that it will make our life uncomfortable, we will not grow from suffering, we will resent it. But if we open our mind to the possibility of a happier, more meaningful life, we can begin to appreciate the challenges. Eventually, we will love Hashem for providing us with the motivation to help us grow.

---

2. We explained this idea in depth in the first mitzvah, *Emunah*, page 78.

We began with the question of how the Torah can command us to feel an emotion. We learn from the *Rishonim* that love for Hashem — like any meaningful form of love — is one that comes from an appreciation of what He is and what He does for us. We can use nature, Torah, and even suffering, to create a burning desire to come close to our Father in Heaven.

II: Excitement for Life

In the *Tochachah* (Admonishment) in *Parashas Ki Savo*, the Torah lists a series of unspeakable catastrophes that will befall our nation if we reject the Torah and mitzvos. In the middle of the account, the Torah states that the tragedies will strike "Because you did not serve Hashem, your God, *amid gladness* and goodness of heart, when everything was abundant" (*Devarim* 28:47).

A question is often raised on this verse. Nowhere in the Torah do we find a mitzvah to be happy. Even the mitzvah of וְשָׂמַחְתָּ בְּחַגֶּךָ, which commands us to be joyous on festivals, is interpreted technically, not emotionally. The Talmud (*Pesachim* 109a) derives from verses in *Tehillim* that meat and wine will make one happy, and that one is therefore required to partake of them on festivals. Nowhere in the Torah do we find a mitzvah to smile — outwardly, or even inwardly. How can we be punished for a sin that we were never warned not to commit?

A similar question can be asked on the verse that states: וּבְיוֹם שִׂמְחַתְכֶם וּבְמוֹעֲדֵיכֶם וּבְרָאשֵׁי חָדְשֵׁכֶם וּתְקַעְתֶּם בַּחֲצֹצְרֹת, *On a day of your gladness, and on your festivals, and on your new moons, you shall sound the trumpets …* (*Bamidbar* 10:10). *Sifri* explains that "a day of your gladness" refers to Shabbos. We know that there is a mitzvah of *oneg* (engaging in pleasurable activities) on Shabbos, but nowhere do we find mention of a mitzvah to be happy on Shabbos. Why does the Torah refer to it as a day of gladness?

⊷§ Happy to Struggle

In order to answer this question, we must take a deeper look at Rambam's explanation of *Ahavas Hashem*. Rambam (*Hilchos Yesodei HaTorah* 2:1) uses some unusual wording in beginning his definition of the mitzvah of *Ahavas Hashem*, stating, *"This glorious and awesome God* — it is a mitzvah to love and fear Him."

"This glorious and awesome God" refers back to the entire first chapter of *Hilchos Yesodei HaTorah*, in which Rambam established exactly Who it is that we believe in. In other words, Rambam is stating, "Remember that Infinite God that you learned about, the One Who created everything, and is Omniscient and Omnipresent? You must love Him."

We have already seen Rambam's teaching that examining nature and appreciating the wisdom with which Hashem created everything will lead us to love Hashem. But together with examining nature, Rambam (ibid. 2:2) suggests that we should also examine *maasav*, Hashem's deeds. Which deeds is Rambam referring to? It seems from the context that he is referring to Creation. He suggests that studying the creatures that Hashem created is insufficient; we must try to understand *why* He created them, and that the answer to that question will lead to intense love of Hashem.

Hashem, the Infinite God, Who lacks nothing, created finite existence *to give to us.* All the beauty, all the wisdom, all the energy — *everything* we see — is for us. Hashem wants us to enjoy the world. This realization should fill us with intense love for Hashem and make us want to draw close to Him.

But there is a problem with this idea. If Hashem wants us to enjoy life, then why do we suffer so much? If we were to choose a lifestyle that we would describe as pleasurable, we would certainly do away with doctor visits and financial woes, to name just a few of the troubles that plague us. Is life really so wonderful?

It is — but only if we are not lazy. Hashem could easily have us breeze through blissful lives without hardships. But He does not want us to be satisfied with the earthly pleasures He created for us in this world. He wants us to receive the ultimate pleasure, to bask in the Glory of His Presence, which we can do only if we develop an appreciation for spiritual pleasure. He gave us the Torah to guide us on how to enjoy this world in a manner that will perfect us so that we can enjoy the Divine Presence. But even that is not enough. As we learned in *Yichud Hashem*,[3] Hashem also challenges us so that we can *earn* closeness to Him, so that we can enjoy it as a reward, not as a gift.

It turns out that every second we spend in this world — even the most painful ones — are for our benefit. And while it is easiest to love Hashem when we derive pleasure in this world, love for Him can carry us through the most difficult moments, too.

> *The Klausenberger Rebbe lost his wife and eleven children during the Holocaust, yet the stories that are told of his actions during and after the Holocaust show how strong his faith and love of Hashem was.*
>
> *Once, in a slave labor camp, he decided that he would not go to work on Simchas Torah, no matter what the consequences would be. When he was absent at roll call, the Nazis sent someone to the barracks to summon him. As punishment for his "crime" and as a warning to his fellow inmates, the Nazis forced him to hold onto a bedframe while several Nazis beat him mercilessly. When they were done, they sent all the prisoners to work, leaving the Rebbe in a bloody heap.*
>
> *The prisoners stumbled about dejectedly that day, certain that they would find their beloved spiritual leader dead when they arrived back at the barracks. To their shock, they found the Rebbe standing up, holding onto the bedframe once again, and moving his feet. As they ran toward him, they noticed that his lips were moving. When they reached him, they realized that the Rebbe had been victorious in his battle with the Nazis. Not only had he survived their beating, but he was dancing and singing in celebration of Simchas Torah, out of a deep love of Hashem for granting us the Torah.*

---

3. Pages 133-135.

Ahavas Hashem is the mitzvah that can encourage us no matter how difficult life becomes. The most basic human instinct, the desire to live, is based on the knowledge that as long as we live we have the potential to come closer to Hashem and to overcome the challenges He sends our way. The mitzvah is, therefore, to develop a passionate love for existence — not for mere physical subsistence, but for the sort of existence we described in the mitzvah of *Emunah*. An *oheiv Hashem* does not drag himself about complaining about his lot in life. He feels that it is great to be alive because he knows what he lives for. He appreciates the opportunity to take part in Hashem's system of growth and be rewarded for his efforts, even if it is painful at times.

We wondered how one could be punished for serving Hashem with a lack of joy if the Torah never commanded us to serve Hashem joyfully. The answer is that the very question is based on mistaken logic. The entire purpose of Torah and mitzvos is to bring us closer to Hashem. One who serves Hashem without joy and emotion achieves little by doing so, because he is not fulfilling the purpose for which he was created.

Furthermore, once we have developed clarity in the purpose of our existence here on earth, we should naturally feel overjoyed when we are presented with opportunities to fulfill our mission. Would we prefer to be like those people who spend their lives chasing various forms of pleasure? Certainly, we who are fortunate enough to serve Hashem should realize that we are among the privileged few, and rejoice at the opportunity He presented to us.

❧ Intellect as an Emotion Builder

We are now able to appreciate a deeper answer to the question we raised at the very beginning of our discussion of *Ahavas Hashem*. We are indeed unlikely to succeed in fulfilling this mitzvah if our efforts are focused on artificially creating such emotions. Just as our efforts in the first three constant mitzvos were rooted in intellect, so too — ideally — our approach to *Ahavas Hashem* should be rooted in intellect. We must use intellect to take *Emunah* to a new level, to come to such intense clarity in the sense of purpose that we feel happy to live, and happy to struggle. *Ahavas Hashem* should make living with *Emunah* our most passionate desire.

The last verse in *Tehillim* is: כֹּל הַנְּשָׁמָה תְּהַלֵּל קָהּ, *every soul praises Hashem* (150:6). *Chazal* (*Bereishis Rabbah* 14:9) add an interpretation, in which the word *neshamah* is read *neshimah*, meaning "breath," thereby turning this verse into a command: Praise Hashem with each breath.

How do you praise Hashem with each breath? Breathing is an involuntary, life-maintaining reflex, but *Chazal* instructed us to be so captivated with life that we turn each involuntary breath into one that we would choose actively if we were given a choice. Each breath should be an expression of, "Life is beautiful, I want more! I want more opportunities to learn. I want more opportunities to grow and perfect myself. I want closeness to Hashem. I want more clarity in His Oneness."

The difference between this constant mitzvah and the others is not in the approach — all are functions of intellect — but in the result. In the first three mitzvos, our intellectual understanding of the mitzvah will create a *mindset*, whereas in *Ahavas Hashem* the intellectual clarity will create emotions.

Ahavas Hashem is a difficult mitzvah to implement. It requires us to look past apparent discomfort and see the greater picture of how suffering helps us grow. But it is also a most beautiful mitzvah. To those who do not have *Ahavas Hashem*, religion may seem like a burden. Instead of being excited about life and Torah, they drag themselves through life thinking, "What can we do — we believe in God, and He says that we are going to be punished if we don't follow His commandments." Not only are they unhappy, but as we have seen, they will also be punished for serving Hashem begrudgingly rather than joyously. If you master this mitzvah, life is great and Torah and mitzvos are best for you. You learn to enjoy every second of life.

❧ Ahavas Hashem: The Active Form

Nearly all 613 mitzvos require some sort of physical action, and even those that do not require action do require specific thought processes. On a superficial level, *Ahavas Hashem*, which is an emotional involvement with Hashem, requires neither of the two. We have seen, however, that the road to the emotional involvement travels through thought and examination of His greatness. In addition, Rambam mentions one concrete action that is associated with *Ahavas Hashem*.

In *Sefer HaMitzvos* (Mitzvah 3), Rambam points out that when people love someone, they cannot contain their excitement over that person. They walk around singing the praises of their beloved day and night, in the hope that all others will realize how wonderful he or she is. The same should hold true for *Ahavas Hashem*, writes Rambam. If you love Hashem, then you should not be able to contain your excitement. You should be walking around singing His praises and trying to convince others to appreciate His greatness and the opportunity He presents.

The question is: What did Rambam intend to teach us by making this comparison. It is clear that he is not suggesting that we teach others about Hashem in order to increase our *own* love for Him. He states that outreach is an *outcome* of our existing love for Hashem. What, then, is the purpose of this comparison?

It appears that Rambam is offering a yardstick with which to measure our progress. If you need to think about sharing religion with others, if you feel that you could easily keep it to yourself, then you have not reached the level of true *Ahavas Hashem*. A true *oheiv Hashem* simply cannot contain himself. He overflows with excitement for Hashem and Torah to the extent that he *must* share it with others. He cannot accept a world in which there are nonbelievers. The thought of humans — and certainly Jews — who are not enamored with Hashem appalls him.

A person who reads this Rambam and comes to the conclusion that he must begin to engage in *kiruv* misses the point. An *oheiv Hashem* is a person who *naturally* feels the need to reach out to those who are unfamiliar with Hashem and Torah, not a person who makes a carefully calculated decision to do so. If you do not feel the burning desire to reach out welling up inside of you, you must first return to the basics. Build up love for Hashem by examining nature, the Torah, and learning to appreciate your challenges. Once you are filled with love for Hashem, the need to teach others will burst forth from you spontaneously.

In our study of *Emunah* we found that sacrificing for *Emunah* serves two functions. On the one hand, it shows that we have *Emunah*, but it also helps us build stronger, more meaningful *Emunah*. The same applies to *Ahavas Hashem*. It is clear from Rambam that we cannot create *Ahavas Hashem* in ourselves merely through teaching others. We must feel at least some degree of that love before we try to teach others. If a person who has such an emotion feels an urge to share it with others, he will find that his own love for Hashem will deepen and intensify as he teaches them.

✑ The "Baruch Hashem" Refrain

Throughout the ages, Jews have flooded formal addresses, and even pointless conversations, with the words *Baruch Hashem*. We also know that in battling a plague that claimed 100 lives each day, King David instituted a rule that we should recite 100 blessings each day (*Bamidbar Rabbah* 18:21). Prayer is one of the primary focuses in the life of a Jew. Rabbi Yochanan, one of the greatest *Amoraim*, goes so far as to exclaim, "If only they would pray all day!" (*Berachos* 21a). Why are Jews obsessed with praying to Hashem and mentioning Him so often?

This question is even stronger when we view it in light of the

Talmudic statements suggesting that too much prayer is not good. The same Rabbi Yochanan ruled that those who devote themselves entirely to Torah study — such as Rabbi Shimon bar Yochai in the years that he spent studying Torah in the cave — should not interrupt their Torah study to pray (*Shabbos* 11a). Moreover, the Talmud (ibid. 10b) states that one who spends too much time in prayer is neglecting eternal pursuits (i.e., Torah study) in favor of temporary ones (prayer is often used to ask for one's material needs).

Is *tefillah* so wonderful that we should pray all day, or can our time be used more efficiently in other pursuits?

Emotions are fragile. They are affected by anything and everything. Even though only major challenges will cause us to forget what we live for, even trivial issues can alter our moods and emotions. How do we maintain our love for Hashem on a *constant* basis? By talking about it. By mentioning Hashem as often as possible, so that He is on our minds day in, day out. By talking to Him when we pray. The *"Baruch Hashem"* inserted into conversation, the *shehakol* blessing before taking a sip of water, are what keep the flame of emotion burning.

But saying *Baruch Hashem* won't work if it is no more than a phrase habitually inserted into conversation. When you say *Baruch Hashem*, mean it. When you recite a blessing, *think* about Hashem and the favor He has granted you by allowing you to eat or drink. The more you focus on Hashem, the more love you will feel for Him.

> *Rabbi Yisrael Salanter was once walking through the streets of a European city when he began to feel extremely thirsty. He walked into a restaurant and ordered a cup of water. When he finished his drink, he walked over to the counter to pay, and was shocked at the astronomical bill they handed him.*
>
> *"All I drank was a cup of water!" he protested.*
>
> *"True," replied the manager, "a cup of water doesn't cost much. But when you drink it in my restaurant, you are paying not only for the water. You are also paying for the ambiance."*

Rav Yisrael later told his students that this story provided him with an answer to a long-standing question he had. When we drink water, we recite the blessing, "Shehakol nihiyeh bid'varo — Everything was created through His utterance." Why do we make such a broad statement when thanking Hashem for some water? Shouldn't such an impressive berachah be reserved for something more significant?

"The restaurant manager answered my question," said Rav Yisrael. "We are not thanking Hashem only for the water. We are thanking Him for the ambiance."

When *Ahavas Hashem* fills a person with a desire for closeness to Hashem, the statements from the Talmud no longer seem contradictory. An *oheiv Hashem* realizes that he cannot spend all day in prayer — because he must also learn what Hashem is all about through Torah study — but he wishes that he could. The relationship with Hashem is so important to him that he would want to spend all day in prayer if it were possible, to get closer and closer to the One he loves so much.

⋞ Don't Lose It!

On a final note, let us examine a statement made by *Chinuch* that seems, at first glance, nearly impossible to implement. *Chinuch* states that when a person focuses on worldly pursuits for their own sake, this will necessarily weaken his love for Hashem. In other words, *Ahavas Hashem* requires us to desire closeness to Hashem to the extent that there is no room for any other desire.

Chinuch is not the only *rishon* to make this point. *Chovos Ha-Levavos* (*Shaar Cheshbon HaNefesh*, Chapter 3) states that spirituality and materialism are *tzaros*, which is a Biblical expression for two women who are married to the same man. The root of *tzaros* is *tzar*, which means *narrow*. When two women share a husband, they constantly compete for a greater portion of their husband's attention and affection, and they always feel as though their share is too small. Every drop of recognition and attention that one wife receives comes at the expense of the other one. Similarly, when a person tries to mix spirituality and materialism, he will find that they constantly compete for his attention, and it will seem as though he is not spending enough time on either pursuit. Indeed, the fact that *Ahavas Hashem* is a constant mitzvah is further proof of the *Chinuch's* statement that materialism is in direct opposition to *Ahavas Hashem*. It is impossible to focus on material pleasure if we are focused on Hashem every second of our life.

The problem is that rejecting materialism appears to exclude us from what we consider normal existence. How is it possible for physical beings, living in such a materialistic environment, to desire nothing other than closeness to Hashem?

If we take a closer look at *Chinuch's* words, we find that it is not as difficult as it seems. He does not say that we lose love for Hashem by taking pleasure from this world or by enjoying His material gifts that He sends us. The question is one of *focus*. Do we *seek* to get our thrills from closeness to Hashem, or from materialism? Do we enjoy food, clothing, and other material pleasures as a means of coming closer to Hashem, or do we enjoy them for their own sake, with the enjoyment being an end in itself?

It is only when we turn our attention away from spirituality and *seek* to develop love for material pleasures that our ability to love Hashem weakens. In the words of *Chovos HaLevavos*, "If your thoughts are on your physical existence, and *all of your attention is focused on it*, then you will neglect your spiritual existence." But as long as our focus is on the pursuit of spirituality, we can — and should — partake of anything we need in order to succeed.

Focusing on spirituality — while realizing that Hashem has created everything in the world for us to enjoy and to grow from, and that He did so in order to reward us with eternal pleasure for our efforts — will infuse us with the excitement and love for life that is *Ahavas Hashem*.

MITZVAH REVIEW

Constant
Mitzvah **4** מצוה
תמידית

אַהֲבַת ה' —
LOVING HASHEM

W e develop love for Hashem when we appreciate His
greatness. Rambam teaches us that we can build that
appreciation by studying nature and Torah, and Ramban adds
that when we act with *mesirus nefesh* and suffer for Hashem's
sake, our love for Him becomes stronger.

We can also build love for Hashem by heightening our
awareness that all of Creation is for our benefit. The vast universe and everything in it, as well as all events and circumstances in history, were created and orchestrated by Hashem
to enable us to use our time in this world to perfect ourselves,
so that we can earn, and therefore enjoy, the reward in the
World to Come.

Practical Applications of Ahavas Hashem

(1) Study nature and Torah as a means of building love for
Hashem. Be sure, however, that you are not blinded
by subconscious feelings that prevent you from seeing the truth. Closeness to Hashem enables you to see
and enjoy the beauty and fulfillment of the Torah's life-

style; don't allow the surface restrictiveness of such a lifestyle to prevent you from giving it a fair chance.

(2) Remind yourself that everything in the world exists for *you*, as a means to help you perfect yourself, so that you can earn and enjoy reward in the World to Come. By doing so, you can turn even the most trying circumstances into positive moments of growth, and you can enjoy life to its fullest.

(3) Talk about Hashem constantly. Insert His Name in conversation to remind you of His Presence in your life. When reciting blessings to thank Him, take a moment to think about the object or occasion you are thanking Him for, and be grateful that He has granted it to you.

(4) Be sure not to diminish your love for Hashem by *actively pursuing* materialism for its own sake.

Additive Effect of Ahavas Hashem

The first three mitzvos, *Emunah*, *Lo Yihiyeh*, and *Yichud Hashem*, focused on developing an understanding of Hashem. In *Emunah* we developed knowledge of His existence; in *Lo Yihiyeh* we came to understand that no other force possesses any power; and in *Yichud Hashem* we expanded that understanding and came to the awareness that no other forces exist at all. *Ahavas Hashem* begins a new set of mitzvos that require us to develop a relationship with Him. In *Ahavas Hashem*, we come to love Him.

In terms of purpose, whereas the first three mitzvos defined what our purpose in life should be — i.e., to perfect ourselves so that we can earn our reward in the World to Come — *Aha-vas Hashem* teaches us to *appreciate* and *enjoy* that opportunity, and to love Hashem for granting it to us.

מִצְוָה תְּמִידִי
CONSTANT MITZVAH
5

יִרְאַת ה'

Fearing Hashem

Dedicated on the occasion
of the engagement of our children

Shiffie Goldenberg to Yoni Merzel

We thank Hakadosh Baruch Hu, who is m'zaveg zivugim. Our joy is boundless and our excitement is palpable. We wish you a life of happiness together and we are certain that the zivug will be oleh yafeh, ahd meah v'esrim shanah together iy"H.

Mazel tov to you, and to Chani & Rikki Grossman, and Devorah & Sammy Merzel.

Love from all of us,
Leon and Agi Goldenberg & the Entire Family

מִצְוַת יִרְאַת ה׳
The Mitzvah to Fear God

לִהְיוֹת יִרְאַת ה׳ עַל פָּנֵינוּ תָּמִיד לְבִלְתִּי נֶחֱטָא, כְּלוֹמַר שֶׁנִּירָא
בִּיאַת עָנְשׁוֹ וְלֹא יִהְיֶה לְבָבֵנוּ בְּלִי מָגוֹר אֵלָיו כָּל הַיּוֹם, וְעַל זֶה
נֶאֱמַר [דברים י, כ], "אֶת ה׳ אֱלֹהֶיךָ תִּירָא".

Fear of Hashem should be reflected on our
countenance constantly, so that we do not sin. That is
to say, we must fear His punishment, and we should
never free our heart of fear of Him for even a moment
of the day, as the verse states, "Hashem, your God, you
shall fear" (*Devarim* 10:20).

(Chinuch, Mitzvah 432)

Constant Mitzvah

5

מצוה תמידית

יִרְאַת ה' — FEARING HASHEM

I: Consequences of Our Actions

DAY 36

The source for the mitzvah to fear Hashem is the verse: אֶת ה' אֱלֹקֶיךָ תִּירָא, *Hashem, your God, you shall fear* (*Devarim* 10:20).

Yiras Hashem, also known as *Yiras Shamayim*, is often translated as *fear of Hashem*, or *fear of Heaven*. When we think of fear, we envision an unbearable — almost paralyzing — emotion that we feel when threatened physically or emotionally. In the context of our relationship with Hashem, this definition is ridiculous. Throughout *Tanach* we find mention of Hashem's overwhelming love for us. We know that Hashem created the world in order to benefit humans. Why should we walk around petrified that He is out to hurt or punish us?

Furthermore, in *Chinuch*'s list of the Six Constant Mitzvos, *Yiras Hashem* immediately follows *Ahavas Hashem*, love of Hashem. The juxtaposition of the two seems contradictory. Is our relationship with Hashem supposed to be a loving one, or are we supposed to live in mortal fear of Him?

A simple answer can be found in Rambam's definition of *Yiras Hashem*, which is not fear, but awe. Rambam (*Hilchos Yesodei Ha-Torah* 2:2) writes that the same realization that should lead us to love God should also cause us to be in awe of Him. We come to love Hashem when we recognize His greatness through the study of the perfection of nature, and that very same appreciation should make us step back in awe when we realize how pitifully meaningless we are in comparison to Him. According to this definition, *yirah* is not *fear* that would cause a person to flee from Hashem. Rather, it is *awe* of Hashem. The closer a person comes to Hashem, the more aware he becomes of the vast difference between the Infinite One and him, and he is overwhelmed with awe.

This answer is insufficient, however, because the Torah often indicates that there *is* a certain aspect of fear involved in this mitzvah. When Avraham Avinu traveled to Philistia to escape a famine, he asked his wife Sarah to tell everyone that she was his sister, for fear they would kill him. When Avimelech, the king, asked him what forced him to do so, he responded: כִּי אָמַרְתִּי רַק אֵין יִרְאַת אֱלֹקִים בַּמָּקוֹם הַזֶּה וַהֲרָגוּנִי עַל דְּבַר אִשְׁתִּי, *Because I said, "**There is but no fear of God in this place** and they will slay me because of my wife"* (*Bereishis* 20:11). Avraham implied that in a place in which there is no fear of God, people will be willing to do anything — even kill — to achieve their goals.

In truth, this point is difficult to understand, even if *yirah* is defined as fear. There are many reasons why a person would not kill even if he does not fear God. There are people who don't believe in God, but would not murder indiscriminately because they are compassionate and merciful. Others refrain from killing out of fear of punishment or revenge. Why would a lack of *Yiras Hashem* make a person likely to murder?

At the other end of the spectrum, a person who is serious about religion, careful in matters of halachah, and deals with honesty, is described as a *"ye'rei Shamayim"* (one who fears Heaven — i.e., Hashem). Such people are not subject to the paralysis normally associated with fear. On the contrary, they are usually active, successful individuals. They do not walk around trembling and wondering when someone — or Someone, as the case may be — will strike them dead. What, then, is true *Yiras Hashem*?

ᵔ§ Natural Consequences of Sin

In order to define *Yiras Hashem*, let us first see how Ran resolves an obvious contradiction.

On one hand, the commandment of לֹא תִקֹּם, *You shall not take revenge*, seems to indicate that taking revenge is a negative trait. In many places, however, Hashem is described as being vengeful: כִּי ה׳ אֱלֹקֶיךָ אֵשׁ אֹכְלָה הוּא אֵל קַנָּא, *For Hashem, your God — He is a consuming fire, a vengeful God* (*Devarim* 4:24); קֵל נְקָמוֹת ה׳ קֵל נְקָמוֹת הוֹפִיעַ, *O God of vengeance, Hashem; O God of vengeance, appear!* (*Tehillim* 94:1). Vengefulness is either objectively right or objectively wrong. How can it be correct for Hashem to be vengeful and wrong for us?

Ran (*Derashah* 10) explains that Hashem is not vengeful in the usual sense of the word. When a human says that he wants to take revenge on someone, he means that he wants to punish that person for angering or offending him. The punishment will often be far worse than the initial wrongdoing, and it will not cause the one who is punished to become better in any way. Hashem does not punish out of anger. When ascribing vengefulness to Hashem, the Torah is expressing itself in a language that humans can understand. What it actually means is that Hashem will punish people in this world for *their own good*, to send them a message that they must improve themselves — or sometimes, in the case of an extremely wicked individual, to make an example of him so that others do not follow in his ways.[1]

---

1. Even in this case, it is in the sinner's best interest that others don't see him as a role model and mimic his sinful behavior, for if they do, he will be held accountable for leading them astray.

Ran then questions his own explanation. Why are souls punished in the afterlife? At that point, the soul can no longer improve its ways, and no one can witness the punishment of a wicked soul and learn not to follow in its path?

Ran's answer to this question provides us with a definition of *Yiras Hashem*.

He explains that Hashem does not decide at random upon punishments in the afterlife. The Talmud (*Bava Kamma* 50a) states that we are not to consider Hashem a *vatran* (tolerant of sin). Why? Because to suggest that Hashem is tolerant of evil is to attribute personality to Him. It suggests that whether or not a person is punished for his sins is dependent on Hashem's mood. It assumes that when the Torah states that something is good, it means that Hashem likes that action and is willing to reward it, and when it characterizes something as evil it means that Hashem dislikes it and therefore punishes for it. But Hashem is Infinite and the laws of the Torah are finite expressions of Hashem's infinity. It is obviously impossible for us to understand how the infinite can be turned into the finite, but that is the very essence of Torah. We need not look any further than the multitude of intricate details contained in each mitzvah for proof of its Infinite Source. No finite being could create such a deep and perfectly harmonious system.

When Hashem wrote in the Torah that something is evil, it means that the action is inherently destructive to the soul. Just as we understand that we cannot drive a car at full speed into a wall and blame the manufacturer for not allowing us and the car to survive the impact, so too, we cannot sin and ask Hashem to look away. The punishment for any sin is an extension of Hashem, and therefore cannot be changed. A soul is punished in the afterlife as an absolute consequence of its sins.

If so, how does the concept of *teshuvah* (repentance) work? Doesn't that seem to indicate that Hashem *does* look aside when a person repents?

Chazal state in many places (see *Tanchuma, Parashas Vayeira* 18) that proper *teshuvah* is so powerful that it erases one's sins so that no stains remain on his soul. Hashem promises us that through *teshuvah*: אִם יִהְיוּ חֲטָאֵיכֶם כַּשָּׁנִים כַּשֶּׁלֶג יַלְבִּינוּ אִם יַאְדִּימוּ כַתּוֹלָע כַּצֶּמֶר יִהְיוּ, *If your sins are like scarlet they will become white as snow, if they have become as red as crimson, they will become [white] like wool* (*Yeshayah* 1:18). This concept so defies nature, that it had to be created before the creation of the natural world (see *Bereishis Rabbah* 1:4).

When one does *teshuvah*, it is not that Hashem ignores the person's sins. He examines the person and finds that there is no sin to punish.

Ran's principle provides a clear definition of *Yiras Hashem*. *Yiras Shamayim* is not an irrational or paralyzing fear of something awful that might happen if we sin. It is a realization that Torah is *real* and unchangeable, that this world is not a free-for-all. If we sin, we will have to pay the price — unless we repent for those sins.

The Talmud (*Yevamos* 121b) teaches that Hashem is "exacting with those close to Him [on issues as insignificant] as a hairsbreadth." This is normally understood to mean that Hashem is stricter with righteous people because He expects more from them. Thus, we find that Hashem reprimanded or punished the patriarchs and other leaders of the Jewish people for sins that were so subtle that the Torah had to present them in exaggerated terms, lest we miss the sinfulness of the action altogether.[2]

---

2. The Torah states, for instance: וַיְהִי בִּשְׁכֹּן יִשְׂרָאֵל בָּאָרֶץ הַהִוא וַיֵּלֶךְ רְאוּבֵן וַיִּשְׁכַּב אֶת בִּלְהָה פִּילֶגֶשׁ אָבִיו, *And it came to pass, while Yisrael dwelt in that land, that Reuven went and lay with Bilhah, his father's concubine* (*Bereishis* 35:22).

The Talmud (*Shabbos* 55b) states that a person who says that Reuven sinned in this story is mistaken. All Reuven actually did was remove his father Yaakov's bed from Bilhah's tent, and place it in his mother Leah's tent. The Torah describes it as a more drastic act, because we would not understand the severity of this deed if it would be presented as it happened.

Similarly, Scripture's depiction (*II Shmuel*, Chapters 11-12) of the incident between King David and Bas-sheva presents it as a grossly immoral act, even as a capital offense.

But the Talmud (ibid. 56a) states once again that one who says that King David sinned is mistaken. Extenuating circumstances in that story enabled him to take

Mesillas Yesharim (Chapter 4) takes the opposite approach. He writes that Hashem is strict with righteous people — *despite* all the love He has for them for their devotion to Him. Hashem's judgment is so precise that even Avraham Avinu — the founder of the Jewish nation — could not be shown leniency. He faltered ever so slightly — so slightly, in fact, that the Sages of the Talmud (*Nedarim* 32a) dispute exactly what it is that he did wrong — and that resulted in the enslavement of his offspring in Egypt for 210 years. The natural consequences of even the smallest of sins are so perfectly precise that they cannot be ignored.

A *ye'rei Shamayim* realizes that when the Torah states that an action is a sin, there are natural consequences that will affect him — and the world at large — should he choose to engage in that action. He also realizes that the only route to success in life is through the Torah, and although other systems seem to work on a temporary basis, they will ultimately lead to failure. And above all, a *ye'rei Shamayim* does not forget about these facts for a second.

ཙ⃰ God Wouldn't Do That!

Beyond resolving the apparent contradiction between the mitzvah to love Hashem and the mitzvah to fear Him, our new definition of *Yiras Hashem* indicates that the two are actually interconnected.

The Torah teaches that when Noach first felt the waters of the *Mabul* (Great Flood) beginning to fall, he did not immediately enter the Ark. He entered only when the intensity of the rainfall forced him to take shelter. The Midrash (cited by *Rashi* to *Bereishis* 7:7) concludes that Noach was among the *ketanai amanah* (those who had limited faith). He believed in God, but he did not believe that He would actually bring such a destructive flood.

This Midrash is astonishing. Noach spend 120 years building

Bas-sheva for a wife legally, but had the *Navi* presented the story as it occurred we would not have seen any iniquity in his actions at all.

the Ark, suffering embarrassment from those around him as he warned them of the approaching disaster. Would he have done so if he felt that his actions were in vain, that Hashem would never really bring a *Mabul*?

The answer lies in the explanation of the contradiction we raised between the mitzvos of *Ahavas Hashem* and *Yiras Hashem*.

When a person instills within himself the idea that Hashem loves him, he puts himself into a dangerous spiritual position. Hashem's love for us can easily be misunderstood as a willingness to look aside when we sin. If Hashem loves me, one can think, then why can't He allow me to act as I see fit? Why must He demand retribution if I transgress His decrees? This sort of outlook on life and religion allows a person to live the life of a sinner, because he is certain that no matter how low he sinks, Hashem will forgive him.

To a lesser degree, this was Noach's mistake. Noach spent 120 years building the Ark because he knew that Hashem was capable of bringing a *Mabul*. He was convinced, however, that Hashem would ultimately forgive humanity's sins out of His deep love for them.

But why do *Chazal* brand Noach a "small believer" for having such thoughts? Is it so terrible to believe that Hashem loves and accepts people for who they are and overlooks their sins because of that love?

The problem with this attitude is that it diminishes the definition of love. Permissiveness does not reflect love. It reflects weakness. A parent who cannot say no to his children is weak, not necessarily loving. A parent who truly loves his children will look out for their best interests, even if the child does not understand the need for the "tough love." When a child falls ill, for instance, a loving parent will force the child to take bitter medicine against all protests.

Hashem created the world through the system called Torah, and He knows that creation can function at its best *only* through that system. If we live with that system, we will succeed in this world, and if we do not, we will fail. *Because* Hashem loves us, *because* He wants us to receive His ultimate goodness, He will not be indifferent if we disobey the laws of the Torah, because that would cause us to lose the reward He has in store for us. When we say that Hashem loves us, then, we mean that He wants only the best for us, and that He will ensure that we receive the ultimate pleasure that only He can provide.

And death does *not* do us part from His love. Hashem created *Gehinnom* (purgatory) for *our* sake, not His. If our souls were forced to spend the rest of eternity with all of the filth that they accumulated in this world, they would be miserable. Out of the deep love Hashem has for us, He ensures that we end up in *Gan Eden* in a condition to enjoy it. Just as our troubles in this world are natural consequences of sins, the purification process of *Gehinnom* cleanses our soul so that we can enjoy *Gan Eden*. Both processes are painful, but they both stem from Hashem's love, not from a need to take revenge.

Ahavas Hashem and *Yiras Hashem* do not contradict each other — on the contrary, they work together. It is because of *Ahavas Hashem*, the mutually loving relationship between Hashem and us, that *Yiras Hashem* is possible. When we realize that Hashem loves us and will ensure that we suffer the natural consequences of our sins so that we can merit the ultimate pleasure of closeness to Him, we can develop a positive outlook toward reward and punishment and develop awe of the One Who considers our deeds and responds to them according to whether or not they are in accordance with His will, thus becoming true *yir'ei Shamayim*.

◄§ True Reality

We have defined *Yiras Shamayim* as an awareness of the absolute nature of the consequences of sin. *Mesillas Yesharim* (Chapter 4) states that there are three levels we can attain, each of which will cause us to focus on a different set of consequences.

Level 1: Punishment

Some people read the Torah's descriptions of suffering that appear in the admonishments (*Tochachah*) or descriptions of *Gehinnom* found in *mussar* works, and they learn to resist temptation because they are afraid of the resultant punishment.

Level 2: Social Status

Others avoid sin out of fear of the damage that will be done to their souls, and the embarrassment they will feel in the World to Come when they are labeled mediocre or worse. They are afraid that they, and all those around them, will compare what they *could* have accomplished to what they *did* accomplish, and the shame of being second-rate will be too much to bear.

While both of these levels — which are similar in that they focus on the negativity of the personal suffering caused by sin — are valid, they are superficial.

Level 3: Lack of Perfection

The third level, while harder to attain, is something to strive for. There are people who avoid sin because they feel such a strong desire to be close to Hashem that they shudder at the mere thought of acting in a way that will distance them from Him. They know that achieving *shleimus* (perfection) is the only way to truly be close to God, and they monitor their actions carefully to ensure that they remain on the road to perfection.

No matter which level one is on, the underlying principle of *Yiras Shamayim* is the same. It is an awareness that moral relativism is a myth. There are absolute rights, and absolute wrongs, and there are consequences for our actions.

Other religions teach that if you have a loving relationship with their deity or deities then you can buy or confess your way out of even the most serious of sins. That is not Judaism. Judaism teaches that you can't buy your way out of sins. The prophets repeatedly warned the Jews who lived in the Temple era that they could not storm into the Temple Courtyard, offer sacrifices, and return home to a lifestyle that ran counter to Hashem's will. Sacrifices offered by people who live their lives with the same lack of spiritual growth and achievement as the animals they sacrifice are worthless. Sacrifices are *part* of a lifestyle. If the sacrifice fits with everything else that one does, it causes Heavenly satisfaction. But one cannot say, "Hashem, look at what I am willing to sacrifice for You. Please let me get away with A, B, and C." No matter how loving a relationship you have with Hashem, you must still follow each of His commandments.

A *ye'rei Shamayim* knows that since right and wrong are not randomly chosen, they cannot be summarily dismissed. Hashem's love for us and ours for Him will not make up for a corrupt or careless lifestyle. Realities remain realities under all circumstances, in all generations, and at all times.

⊷§ "It's Not So Bad"

Let us look at a practical application of our definition of *Yiras Shamayim*, and then return to a question we asked at the beginning of our study.

Shulchan Aruch (*Orach Chaim* 32:20) rules that a *sofer* (scribe) who writes *tefillin* must be a *ye'rei Shamayim*. Why? Because the tiniest, most subtle mistakes can invalidate the *tefillin*, and only certain types of mistakes may be repaired. A *sofer* invests much time into writing each *parashah*. If he is not a *ye'rei Shamayim*, he will be tempted to fix mistakes that have made the *tefillin* nonkosher, and sell them as perfectly kosher *tefillin*. The buyer can never know the difference.

It would seem that a *sofer* who sells nonkosher *tefillin* is a thief, not just lacking in *Yiras Shamayim*. Why does *Shulchan Aruch* emphasize the need for a *ye'rei Shamayim*.

The difference between an acceptable repair and a prohibited one can be very small. The ethical dilemma that a *sofer* faces is not whether or not to cheat. No *sofer* — unless he is dishonest — would consider making a repair to *tefillin* that were absolutely, irreparably nonkosher. The dilemma arises when the problem is in a grey area of halachah. When faced with a choice of repairing something that can be ruled either way, the overwhelming concern in a *ye'rei Shamayim*'s mind will be the consequence of sin. He will choose to get rid of a *parashah* that took hours to write rather than take a chance. A *sofer* with less *Yiras Shamayim* will say to himself, "Look, it is borderline. If you don't look *very* closely it looks fine, and it's okay to make the repair." Does he think that he is cheating the potential consumer? No. But his lack of *Yiras Shamayim* causes him to define halachah to suit his interests, and allows him to act in a way that a *ye'rei Shamayim* would not. The same applies to a *shochet*, a cook, or a businessman. We are all likely to decide questionable issues in our favor. It takes *Yiras Shamayim* to prevent us from doing so.

If we learn a lesson from this example, we can understand why Avraham Avinu felt that the Philistines' lack of *Yiras Shamayim* might lead them to murder him. When a person's principles are flexible, when his ethical compass is weakened by lack of seriousness toward the spiritual reality of mitzvos and sins, he will redefine the rules to meet his personal interests. Avraham Avinu realized that this tendency to rationalize in order to justify whatever is in one's personal self-interest can eventually lead to murder.

This realization is one that we can identify with easily in our times. A Princeton bioethics professor, considered one of the world's leading "ethicists," advocates redefining "life" to permit killing infants that are "defective," even until the age of 3. He also proposes that doctors be allowed to terminate the lives of patients who are unable to make their own decisions due to dementia or loss of consciousness, as long as the doctor thinks that the patient would have preferred to die under such circumstances. In addition, several countries now allow "death with dignity," in which a doctor helps a patient commit suicide. These trends almost always come together — as is the case with the Princeton professor — with an outlook on the world that places humans in the same category as animals, thus allowing humans to behave without any ethical compass whatsoever.

Avraham Avinu taught us that a *ye'rei Shamayim* accepts the Torah's definition of murder. A non-*ye'rei Shamayim* may redefine murder to make it permissible in cases in which he can derive personal gain from the act.

◈ Fear Yourself

To summarize, we defined *Yiras Hashem* as taking Hashem and Torah seriously. But don't we have to take Him seriously in order to love Him? Why is this a definition for the mitzvah of *Yirah* and not *Ahavah*?

We found that *Ahavas Hashem* meant to be excited and enthralled with life. It is easy to take Hashem seriously in the context of *ahavah*, because we can create an image of Him that is lovable. A person can easily become happy-go-lucky, walking around with a smug sense of satisfaction with life that he attributes to *bitachon*. But true *Ahavas Hashem* is not about being carefree and lighthearted. If it is not combined with *Yiras Hashem*, it is deficient. *Yirah* requires us to make sure that the image of God that we are taking seriously is His *true* image. It means understanding who God is, what He expects of us, how difficult it can be to follow His commandments — and loving life nonetheless. It means realizing that the struggle is beautiful, because it allows us to choose — and earn — eternal pleasure, and it also contains the realization that we can choose eternal suffering. *Ahavah* coupled with *Yirah* means that we recognize the gravity of each decision we make, but that we are thrilled to be able to make those decisions.

The Talmud (*Berachos* 60a) relates that a student was once following Rabbi Yishmael bar Rav Yosi through the market of Zion, and Rabbi Yishmael noticed that the student was fearful. "You are a

202 ∾ CONSTANT MITZVAH 5: FEARING HASHEM

sinner," Rabbi Yishmael said, "for the verse states: פָּחֲדוּ בְצִיּוֹן חַטָּאִים, *Those who are fearful in Zion are sinners (Yeshayah 33:14)."*

"But another verse states: אַשְׁרֵי אָדָם מְפַחֵד תָּמִיד, *Praiseworthy is the man who always fears (Mishlei 28:14)*," protested the student.

"That verse refers to Torah matters," replied Rabbi Yishmael.

When you feel fearful, you must identify the source of the fear. Are you afraid of misfortune? A foreign invasion? Disease? Losing money? *Pachadu b'Zion chataim.* Fear brought on by such issues is wrong. It stems from attributing far too much significance to this world. It is a consequence of a distorted understanding of our mission that leads people to believe that physical, emotional, and financial security in *this* world is what really matters. "Those who fear in Zion are sinners" because the material world means so much to them that the mere possibility of trouble causes them to worry. They have forgotten that God loves us — *always*, that He is not going to abandon us, and that He challenges us because He knows that we need it for our spiritual growth.

We don't ask to be challenged, but there is no reason to fear challenges if we realize that Hashem is behind them. There may be suspense. We don't know how things will turn out. But we do know that however they turn out, it will be for the best. In regard to the material world, then, fear is wrong.

When King Shlomo said, "Praiseworthy is the man who always fears," what fear was he referring to? The fear of what we can do to ourselves. Fear that we can waste our lives. Fear that we will pass up all the opportunities for growth that Hashem provides for us. Such fear comes from the realization that Hashem will allow us to make a mess of our lives if we choose to do so. He will allow us to use our talents to pursue silly, meaningless goals.

If there is something to fear, it is yourself. We call that fear *Yiras Shamayim,* fear of Heaven, because in order to fear yourself you must believe that there are consequences to your actions, that there is a system of right and wrong, and a Judge watching your every decision and action. If you believe that God loves you so much that

He will look aside as you waste your life, then you will not succeed. Fear of Heaven means that you realize that Hashem created a system of reward and punishment, and that there are no loopholes. He does not want you to commit spiritual suicide, but He will not prevent you from doing so, because He provided you with free will. If you use that free will to ruin your own life, He will not stop you. He will try to get your attention and send you messages from time to time, but it is ultimately up to you to choose correctly and act correctly.

If there is something to fear, it is not what will happen in the material world. Don't fear disease. Don't fear financial woes. Those are challenges that can help you grow. Fear spiritual disaster. Fear the fact that if you want to make a mess of your life, no one will stop you. Fear what you can do to yourself if you don't take part in Hashem's system.

Fear yourself.

⤧ Two Sets of Keys

In *Yichud Hashem* we learned that only those who work in this world to earn their reward in the World to Come will be able to enjoy it. Fear of Heaven takes that concept one step further. It teaches us that each of our actions has consequences, and that Hashem *will not* look aside and allow us to sin and then reward us with eternal pleasure, because we won't enjoy it.

In answer to our question, then, love of Hashem does not contradict fear of Him — on the contrary, true love of Hashem can exist only when it is coupled with fear. If we see Hashem as a compassionate, devoted Father Who will allow us to do whatever we want, then we do not love Him. True love of Hashem stems from the realization that His entire system of reward and punishment is for our benefit — *including* the free will to make a mess of our lives. It is all there to enable us to earn eternal pleasure on our own.

Love of Hashem stems from the knowledge that He has placed

the keys to eternal pleasure in our hands. Fear of Hashem stems from the knowledge that He has also handed us the keys to eternal disappointment.

II: Living With a Cheshbon

The theoretical definition of *Yiras Hashem* is to take Hashem, the Torah, and the consequences of our actions seriously. We must now focus on how to implement *Yiras Shamayim* on a practical level. It is clear from many sources — most of all Ramchal in *Mesillas Yesharim* — that in order to build *Yiras Shamayim*, one must begin to work with a *cheshbon hanefesh* (lit., calculation of the soul). Let us look at the steps outlined by Ramchal and see how they will help us attain *Yiras Shamayim*.

◆§ Where Are You Headed?

When a person sets out on a journey, the first thing he must choose is a destination. Similarly, in planning our spiritual path through life, we must first have a clear definition of our life goals. The Six Constant Mitzvos define them for us. In *Emunah* we learn that we are here for a purpose — to perfect ourselves and the world around us, so that we can enjoy the ultimate pleasure of basking in Hashem's Presence in the World to Come. In *Lo Yihiyeh* we learn that there is no other method to succeed in this world. In *Yichud Hashem* we learn that every aspect of Creation and every event in our life was placed there by Hashem to help us succeed in our mission. *Ahavas Hashem* requires us to be excited and take pleasure in our share in the purpose of Creation, and *Yiras Hashem* requires us to realize that Torah is real, and that every one of our actions will draw a consequence.

It is extremely important to clarify those ideals before moving on to their practical application. There are people for whom Judaism and Torah means avoiding *issurim* (prohibitions). They spend their lives trying not to transgress halachah. Their approach calls for eternal *mesirus nefesh* (self-sacrifice). They avoid this prohibition, and that one, and the other one, and eventually it starts to get difficult. They want to make money, for instance, but religion keeps getting in their way. They must close their businesses on Shabbos, there are investments that are halachically unacceptable, and there are all sorts of business laws they must comply with because halachah requires us to be honest. Eventually they resent the constant burden of halachah and start looking for loopholes. And if there are no loopholes, they create them. Thus we find people shopping for lenient opinions. You hear statements such as, "There must be some *posek* (halachic authority) who will allow it," or "I heard that someone said it is permissible to claim this sort of deduction." And if all else fails, there is the greatest cop-out of all: "I'm not so *frum* (righteous)."

When people set personal goals and then try to make halachah conform to those goals, life becomes one long effort to survive the nuisance called halachah. Even those who do not crack and manage to live a life of sacrifice are missing the point. Torah is not something you learn to live *with* — it's what you live *for*.

Another group of people focuses only on the positive mitzvos of the Torah. Some people are constantly talking about the need for *ahavas Yisrael* (love of fellow Jews), for instance, even while they violate negative commandments — such as slandering those who they feel do not have *ahavas Yisrael* — to achieve their goals.

Yet another group pursues *chumros*, halachic stringencies that may or may not be necessary, as a means of feeling as if they are sacrificing for Hashem's sake. While their search for holiness is praiseworthy, it can often come at a cost to others, and it can also be a diversionary tactic set in place by the *yetzer hara* to cause a person to focus on technicalities rather than on true spiritual advancement.

The first aspect of *cheshbon hanefesh*, then, is to ask yourself, "What do I live for? Do I turn to Torah for direction, or do I set my goals and then make sure that Torah does not interfere? Why do

I pursue certain mitzvos over others? Why do I choose to adopt stringencies in halachah?"

If *Yiras Hashem* means taking Torah seriously and realizing that it is a reality, then developing *Yiras Hashem* requires us to take an honest look at our lives and make sure that Torah is our goal, not something that must conform to our goals.

◄§ How Will You Get There?

Taking our analogy one step further, when a traveler has decided on a destination, he must then figure out how to reach his destination. In our spiritual journey, too, we must develop a plan of how to carry out our goals. This step is defined in the Torah as *Yiras Shamayim*.

The Biblical nation of Amalek is referred to in the Torah as לֹא יָרֵא אֱלֹקִים, a nation that did not fear God.[3] After the Jews left Egypt, no nation was willing to challenge them. The entire world heard about the terrible plagues that had struck the Egyptians and of the splitting of the Sea of Reeds, and they were all petrified: שָׁמְעוּ עַמִּים יִרְגָּזוּן חִיל אָחַז יֹשְׁבֵי פְּלָשֶׁת, *Peoples heard — they were agitated; terror gripped the dwellers of Philistia* (*Shemos* 15:14). The nations knew that the Jews were traveling to the Land of Israel, and they were certain that no one could stand in their way. One nation was unimpressed: Amalek. Everyone was afraid of God's Mighty Hand, except for Amalek. They lost the battle, but they had dared to fight. They didn't take God seriously.

Amalek were descendants of Eisav. The Talmud (*Sotah* 13a) and *Pirkei D'Rabbi Eliezer* (38) teach that when the tribes brought Yaakov's coffin to *Me'aras HaMachpelah* for burial, Eisav protested that the spot belonged to him. He argued that the cave had been purchased by Avraham Avinu as a family burial spot, and since Yaakov had already used one of two remaining spots to bury Leah,

---

3. *Devarim* 25:18.

the other one belonged to him (Eisav). One of Yaakov's grandsons, who was a deaf-mute, could not understand why the burial was being delayed. When the others indicated that Eisav was the cause, he took a shovel and chopped off Eisav's head. It rolled into the *Me'aras HaMachpelah* and remains there until this very day.

Commentators explain that this event was not accidental. Eisav's head *belonged* in *Mearas HaMachpelah*, because as far as his intellect was concerned — Eisav was on the level of a patriarch. He had the understanding — even the clarity — of a patriarch. But Eisav suffered from "transmission failure." There was no connection between his mind and the rest of his body. He knew what was right, but he was still Eisav: a thief, philanderer, and murderer. That trait was passed on to Amalek, who knew that they would lose the war with the Jews, but fought anyway. And that is described by the Torah as *lo yir'ei Elokim*. A person who knows the truth but does not implement it does not fear God.

The second step in *Yiras Shamayim* is to take the goals you have defined for yourself in step one and implement them. Make sure that your mind and your body are connected, that your behavior mirrors your perception of truth. Each time you act, make sure that the action you want to take fits into your life goal and will bring you closer to the purpose for which you were created.

This step of *cheshbon* is the most difficult one, because in the heat of the moment we are influenced by so many outside circumstances that it is almost impossible to think clearly. We are torn between two or more options that pull us in opposite directions. We have desires that make us feel as though we absolutely *must* act, and we also have a tendency toward justifying our actions and making ourselves feel that acting on our desires is best for us. Such human weakness can easily overpower our knowledge of right and wrong. We try our best to weigh our options objectively, but how do we know whether we are choosing correctly?

❧ Cheshbon in the Aftermath

Hindsight, they say, is 20-20. We are biased when we make our decisions, but in the aftermath, less so. Once we have acted upon our decisions, there is a good chance that we will know whether we were right or wrong. Each one of us has experienced this. We have had situations when we thought we were doing something great, and we realized afterward that it was terrible. The bias often disappears in the aftermath.

On one level, this will allow us to repent and repair the damage we have done. On a much deeper level, it should cause us to examine not only the erroneous *action*, but also what led to the mistake. Everyone makes mistakes, but if our decision-making process is defective, then we will continue to err indefinitely.

This part of *cheshbon hanefesh* is unique in that it is not one that we calculate on a scheduled basis. The other portions of *cheshbon hanefesh* should be performed on schedule. Each person must choose a schedule that will work for him — once a day, once a week, or at *least* once a month — and stick to it faithfully. Decision-making processes, however, need not be examined regularly. It is when we find ourselves regretting an action that we initially considered proper that we must examine the thought process that caused us to err. We must ask ourselves whether the mistaken decision was a glitch, or a representative sample of our decision-making process. If it was the latter, then we must redefine our goals and strengthen our commitment to what we know to be true.

❧ Too Much Cheshbon: The Yetzer Hara's Goal

From the *yetzer hara*'s standpoint, the most dangerous opponents are those who perform a *cheshbon hanefesh* regularly. He knows that those who plan their goals carefully, follow through in action, and then reexamine to ensure that they are living up to their expectations of themselves, will make themselves resistant to his seduction. When a person begins to keep a *cheshbon hanefesh*, the *yetzer hara* will place every possible obstacle in his path to try to stop him. The only defense is to be informed and cautious.

The main obstacle the *yetzer hara* uses is the temptation toward overdoing *cheshbon*. Like everything else, *cheshbon hanefesh* can be a double-edged sword. The potential for growth is immense, but you can also *cheshbon* yourself into paralysis. If you start from scratch each day, examining over and over again what you live for, you will never amount to much. If you find yourself wondering over and over whether to act in a way that you already determined to be sinful in the past, then the *yetzer hara* has trapped you. He is paralyzing you and preventing you from moving on to greater issues. Such contemplation may seem like *Yiras Shamayim*, but it is not. It is the *yetzer hara* making sure that you are unable to do anything of value, because you are too busy thinking and planning.

How do you know when you are doing enough *cheshbon hanefesh*, and when you are overdoing it? Once again, it is only in the aftermath that it will become clear. The right amount of *cheshbon hanefesh* should enable you to attain your goals. If you are consistently planning goals and are unable to follow through in action, you probably are not spending enough time planning on how best to follow through. On the other hand, if you look back and find that you have spent much time in the thinking and planning phase but did not take action, then you are substituting *cheshbon* for action.

How do you find the golden mean? Like everything else in life, you must use your judgment and learn from experience. No one can quantify the amount of *cheshbon hanefesh* that you need to do or tell you how much time to spend on each phase. You must learn to evaluate your own tendencies. Do you have a tendency to proceed on a course of action without evaluating it as you go along, only catching yourself 300 steps down the road wondering how you got there? If so, make sure to take stock of your actions more carefully.

But on the other hand, as noted above, be just as cautious of getting caught-up in *cheshbon hanefesh*.

The only clear-cut rule is that life goals — as well as the general route to achieve them — should not be reevaluated every day. If you try something new every day, or if you alternate between two options, then you cannot make any progress. You must choose a goal and a path with which to achieve it, and stick to it for a while before reconsidering. If you have two good choices, always choose the less demanding of the two so that you can pursue it consistently. There is little to gain and much to lose by reaching for the more difficult level. Inconsistency is more dangerous than slight underachievement. You can always move up to a more demanding level after succeeding at that lower level for a while, but if you overextend yourself at the start, you might become so frustrated by your lack of success that you will abandon your goals altogether. Choose a specific amount of time that you will stick to your path and your goal before reconsidering, and only reevaluate when the trial period has run its course.

At the same time, however, you must be sure that consistency is not making you numb and causing you to act out of rote. It is important to maintain freshness by reviewing and reminding yourself of your goals regularly.

Rabbi Samson Raphael Hirsch poses an interesting question on the first service practiced daily in the *Beis HaMikdash*. Each day, as the Kohanim prepared the Altar for the daily offering, they would take a bit of the accumulated ash from the previous day and place it next to the Altar.[4] Generally speaking, however, we were not supposed to use "leftovers" in the *Beis HaMikdash*, notes Rav Hirsch. Water left in the *Kiyor* (Laver) overnight, for instance, was not fit for use for washing the Kohanim's hands and feet the next morning. Why, then, asks Rav Hirsch, did the very first service

---

4. This was not done to cleanse the Altar; the excess ashes were removed entirely from the Courtyard. The placement of a small amount of ash next to the Altar was a sacred service in its own right.

involve taking old ashes and depositing them next to the Altar?

We must begin with a fresh start each day, explains Rav Hirsch, because there is a need for energy in the service of Hashem. We should not serve Hashem in a certain manner today just because we did so yesterday. We must live according to our current understanding of right and wrong, not rehash the — perhaps mistaken — beliefs and decisions of yesteryear. But while beginning our service with freshness each morning, continues Rav Hirsch, we must realize that we need not discard the old in order to bring in the new. We place some of yesterday's ash next to the Altar each morning before proceeding to today's *avodah* (service) to show that today's achievements must be built *upon* yesterday's, not in place of them.

> At Chassidic weddings, it is customary to have a badchan (jester) entertain the groom and bride. A badchan once asked Rav Yoel Teitelbaum, the Satmar Rav, for permission to imitate his unique style of prayer. The Rebbe, a witty man, readily agreed.
>
> As the badchan went through his routine, he noticed that tears started to roll down the Rebbe's face. He cut his act short, and ran over to the Rebbe to apologize. "I didn't mean to be disrespectful," he stammered. "I specifically approached the Rebbe to ask for permission because I did not want to hurt his feelings."
>
> "I am not crying because I was insulted," the Rebbe responded. "I am crying because I realized that my manner of prayer must be extremely consistent for you to be able to imitate me so well. If others are able to mimic me so perfectly, perhaps I am also mimicking myself."

This idea is appropriate for all aspects of service of Hashem, but especially to *cheshbon hanefesh*. If you erase the past and start from square one each day, you will spend your entire life on square one. Learn from yesterday's mistakes, but make sure to continue climbing today, not go back to ground level. Trust your previous decisions. Once you have decided what you live for, stick with it, unless you have reason to believe that you erred in that decision. Don't constantly doubt and reevaluate your life goals as part of your regular *cheshbon hanefesh*, or you will *cheshbon* yourself to death.

And the same is true for *cheshbon hanefesh* regarding your actions and motives. You must question your every action and your every motive. But then you must also question your questioning. Are you really growing through such careful scrutiny, or have you subconsciously determined that if you allow common sense to limit the amount of time you spend on *cheshbon hanefesh*, you will have to make tough demands of yourself? The *yetzer hara* can hijack *cheshbon hanefesh* and cause you to scrutinize and doubt every action and decision so that he can paralyze you and prevent you from real growth. In extreme cases, people have even mistaken laziness for *cheshbon*-induced paralysis, thus turning *cheshbon hanefesh* into an obstacle to growth.

↜§ Yirah in Action

As much as *Yiras Shamayim* is about planning and accounting, we must realize that the most carefully laid plans for spiritual perfection can often be ruined by bad habits and tendencies, or lifestyle decisions that force us to act in a certain way. It is therefore important to discuss the most basic form of *Yiras Shamayim*: the need to be on guard at all times.

A *ye'rei Shamayim* realizes that once the adrenaline starts to flow, it will be nearly impossible to avoid sin. It is easy to get to the point of no return. Once you have lost your temper, for instance, it is hard to stop yourself from saying something harmful, even if you know that it is wrong. The objective is to catch yourself one step earlier, when you are still able to control yourself.

We have questioned[5] how a human being is capable of fulfilling six mitzvos each second and still lead a productive life, and we

---

5. See Introduction, pages 41-43, and the mitzvah of *Emunah*, pages 68-69.

explained that constant mitzvos are supposed to form an attitude that is present in our subconscious mind at all times. We fulfill these mitzvos by developing the correct outlook on life through studying them and thinking about them, and then reflecting that outlook in our actions constantly.

In that context, *Yiras Shamayim* requires us to decide that when we are tempted to sin, we will have a little red light go on in our mind and remind us that we are being tested. Once we have our goals clearly defined, this warning lamp will declare, "Stop! This is bad for you. This is not what you should be doing. This is not what you believe in. You understand the natural consequences of this action, and you don't really want to do this."

In short, a *ye'rei Shamayim* is a person who is in total control: in control of his thoughts, in control of his goals, and most importantly, in control of his behavior.

III: Be Honest With Yourself

If *cheshbon hanefesh* is one of the great building blocks of *Yiras Hashem*, its foundation is honesty. A person who is not honest with himself can justify plans and actions that are the furthest thing from *avodas Hashem*; a person who is honest with himself will not.

⇜§ Don't Be a Spectator

One of the first things we must realize is that we are constantly making choices. There are times when we feel that we are just breezing through life on cruise control, but in reality we keep making choices. Every time we act — and every time we *don't* act — we have made a decision, even if the "decision" is to maintain our momentum and not reconsider what we are doing. And as we have come to learn, those choices will bear consequences — natural consequences that cannot be avoided. Don't be an observer in your life. Participate in it. Realize that you are choosing priorities in everything you do, and everything you don't do. Be aware of the constant battle with the *yetzer hara*. Be conscious of his ever-present influence in your life. Even Torah study — the ultimate pursuit — might be sanctioned by the *yetzer hara*. You must stop and ask yourself from time to time, "Why do I study Torah?" If the answer is because you are seeking truth, great. But perhaps you know the truth, and you study now because you enjoy the mental exercise. Or perhaps you are studying because it is easier to study truth than to implement it in your life. Or maybe you are merely floating along with the tide in your school, shul, or home, but with little belief and emotion in what you are doing.

To fear Hashem means to evaluate yourself according to His standards, and to realize that there is no way to fool Him. Be honest with yourself before you embark on any endeavor. Make sure that you are aware of the motives that are fueling your interest in that endeavor, and that they are harmonious with your life goals.

ᴈ§ Perfect Precision

We have defined *Yiras Hashem* as an awareness of the natural consequences of our actions. Just as Hashem created all of nature with perfect precision, the natural consequences of our actions are also perfectly precise. This requires us to be extremely aware of our motives — whether primary, secondary, or third level. We must realize that Hashem will reward or punish us not only for the primary motives of our actions, but also for the secondary and third-level motives as well.

> *The Rebbe of Alexander was once insulted verbally at a gathering in his Chassidic court. His attacker hurled insult after insult at the Rebbe, who remained silent the entire time.*
>
> *Later, a Chassid asked the Rebbe why he had not excommunicated the man for the gross violation of the Torah's honor, as mandated by halachah.*
>
> *"I know that the man deserved to be excommunicated," replied the Rebbe, "but I was worried that I might derive a small measure of satisfaction from meting out the punishment. I might have been defending my personal honor, not the Torah's."*
>
> *Great man that he was, the Rebbe evaluated himself objectively. Knowing that the propriety of punishing the sinner might be tainted by the satisfaction of humbling his abuser, he chose to refrain.*

The system of reward and punishment is so precise that it takes into account minute details and emotions. If a person is unable to withstand temptation but feels terrible as he commits a sin, the damage to his soul will not be as devastating as it would be if he had committed it with enthusiasm. The system is so precise that not only is each emotion accounted for, but the intensity of the emotion is also measured. A person who feels a bit of discomfort with himself will have that measure of discomfort deducted from his sin, and someone who could not control himself but is overcome by guilt will have more deducted.

The same is true in the reverse. If a person hurts someone in his excitement to perform a mitzvah, that will be counted as an imperfection in his mitzvah. Hashem will not overlook the pain he caused out of deference to the praiseworthy act.

Our motives are also a factor in the equation. Why do we perform mitzvos? Humans are complex. We can have several motives for each decision and action. If we are honest with ourselves, we might find ourselves guilty of seeking glory for performing mitzvos. And even if we begin a mitzvah with the purest intentions, but we then notice someone watching us and we appreciate that attention, we lose some of the reward. On the positive side, every ounce of energy invested into mitzvos is credited. No detail is too insignificant for Hashem to consider.

> *The Brisker Rav told Rav Shach a story that had been transmitted from generation to generation in his family, dating back to Rabbi Chaim of Volozhin, who was a disciple of the Gaon of Vilna.*
>
> *The Gaon's wife and a close friend would collect charity in Vilna. They spent many hours together, walking from door to door to obtain funds for the poor. They made an agreement with each other: the first of the two to pass on would come to the other one in a dream and relate how her judgment went in the Heavenly Court.*
>
> *The other woman died first, and after a while she came to the Gaon's wife in a dream. "I am not allowed to divulge much information about the Heavenly Court," she said, "but since I agreed to come back to you in a dream, they have allowed me to divulge one detail.*

"One day, when we were out collecting," she continued, *"we visited a certain woman's home, only to find that she was out. Then you noticed her walking on the other side of the street. You raised your hand to point out to me that she was there, and we crossed the street together and received a contribution from her.*

"When the Heavenly Court was reviewing my mitzvos, I saw that the amount of money we received from her appeared on both of our records, because we both worked equally hard to collect it. Each step that we took toward the woman's house, and the steps we took when we crossed the street, also appeared on both our records. There is one action, however, for which only you will receive credit. The effort you expended by raising your arm and pointing to the woman on the other side of the street will be an eternal credit on your behalf."

We are only human, and it is impossible to act selflessly when we are young and immature. If we are not honest with ourselves, we can go through life performing mitzvos with the same childish, ulterior motives that we had when we were young. *Yiras Shamayim* will allow us to evaluate our progress and determine whether we are growing in terms of the purity of our intentions while studying Torah and performing mitzvos.

◆§ Know Thyself

The Torah often concludes sections dealing with interactions with others with the words: וְיָרֵאתָ מֵאֱלֹקֶיךָ אֲנִי ה', *fear your God, I am Hashem* (*Vayikra* 19:14,32; 25:17,36,43). Perhaps this is because the area of interpersonal relationships is one in which *Yiras Shamayim* is crucial. Often we are called upon to help others. Sometimes we are truly unable to help. But there are situations in which we *can* help, but we find ways to make it seem as though we are unable to.

Legend has it that there was a man who fooled all of Warsaw. Whenever he introduced himself to someone he said that his name is Shmerel. Finally, on his deathbed, he told all of his friends, "You see, I fooled you all. My name was really Berel, and you all thought that I was Shmerel."

As ridiculous as this sounds, the *baalei mussar* would point out that we all do this to a certain extent. We make every effort to present ourselves as righteous individuals. Whom are we fooling? Ourselves.

Yiras Shamayim should bring a realization that you can convince people that you have no time for them, and no time for your family, but ultimately, you will pay the price. You may succeed in fooling the world — just as good old Berel did — but if you neglect your soul, if you neglect your family, if you neglect others, you hurt yourself more than anyone else. Realize that life is not about impressing people. You might have them fooled, but you, and only you, truly lose out.

By concluding mitzvos that deal with interpersonal relationships with "fear your God," the Torah is teaching that if you are not in the mood of helping someone, admit it. If not to them, at least to yourself. Hashem knows the truth, and your best chance for success in this world is to know the truth yourself. If you are honest with yourself, you can eventually train yourself to be available for others. If you constantly justify your actions to yourself, you are likely to continue in the path of self-justification forever.

The same holds true in all areas of life. Ignorance is not bliss; knowledge is of utmost importance. This is especially true when it comes to your sense of reality. When you are doing something wrong, admit it to yourself. If you pervert your sense of reality in small issues, you will train yourself to justify the worst sins. A person who commits a sin and knows that he is doing something wrong is much better off than one who justifies it and thinks that he is innocent. There is hope for the former. His feeling of guilt will motivate him to repent and build his resistance to temptation so that he can survive the next onslaught. A person who feels that he is innocent will repeat his sins over and over without feeling sorry, and will eventually move on to worse sins. Once his sense of reality is warped, it is hard for him to stop.

₰ Honesty: Taking Control

The observant Jew who lacks *Yiras Shamayim* loses his sense of reality quite easily. *Yiras Shamayim* can be measured by the amount one is willing to sacrifice — either in terms of money, exertion, or embarrassment — before he begins to bend halachah. When you know something is wrong, but you feel that you must do it anyway because to desist will cost you money, or you will have to exert yourself, or you will be embarrassed, then your sense of reality is slipping.

Honesty will help you take control in such situations. If you are tempted to cheat in business, for instance, take the advice of the Mishnah in *Avos* (2:1): "Calculate the pleasure of the sin against the suffering." You think that you are going to get rich by stealing? Be honest: you don't really *want* to be rich. You want to be happy. How will you feel for the rest of your life knowing that you cheated someone? Aside from the damage you are doing to your soul in the World to Come, what is it going to be like *in this world* to have to keep lying and lying to cover up for what you did? Will cheating truly bring you happiness?

Fear of God means recognizing the consequences not only in the next world, but also in this one. If it is wrong, it is wrong in both worlds. Realize that sin is the result of extreme shortsightedness. It may be difficult to pass up temporary pleasure, but ultimately, when you do something that you know is wrong, you feel horrible afterward. Be honest with yourself, know your true goals, and take control.

❧ Loving the Fear

We began this mitzvah by raising an apparent contradiction between *Ahavas Hashem* and *Yiras Hashem*. Although we have seen several answers along the way, we can now add one that sums up all that we have seen in the mitzvos of *Ahavah* and *Yirah*.

Ahavah, in our definition, was about loving and enjoying the system that Hashem developed for our personal growth and development. In *Yirah* we learn *how* to enjoy life. True happiness can be achieved only when you realize that there are consequences to your actions, and you identify the talents that Hashem gave you and use them for the correct purpose. True enjoyment of life comes from being tough on yourself, from forcing yourself to scrutinize every action and every motive — and then scrutinizing the scrutiny to make sure that you are not paralyzing yourself by being overly critical.

And happiness comes from being honest with yourself. Know when you are doing something meaningful. And when you are making an effort to convince everyone — yourself included — that you are engaged in some great and holy endeavor, but you are actually wasting time, recognize that unpleasant fact. Know when your Torah study, and all your other efforts to serve Hashem, are focused on the correct goals, and recognize when you are using them as an excuse to evade responsibility for those around you. Know when your soul-searching is causing you to grow, and recognize when it is just a lazy way of getting out of doing anything meaningful.

It is difficult to be so brutally honest with ourselves, but it is also enjoyable, because it is fascinating. What our subconscious mind can do is fascinating. Peeling away layer after layer of motives and exposing the true reasons for our actions may be difficult, but we will be much happier when we get to the truth.

Yiras Hashem is not to tremble. Fear of God is to realize that there are consequences to our actions, and that there is precision. We do not live with the attitude of, "Eat, drink, and be merry, for tomorrow you die." We are concerned with each and every action, because we know that we are capable of making a mess of our life — but we are also capable of making a masterpiece of our life.

When we wrote that *Ahavas Hashem* is about enjoying life, we did not mean that one should become carefree and blithe. God placed us into a system in which we can earn our eternal reward by succeeding in handling the challenges He places before us, but we can also make a mess of our life — and we must take those implications seriously.

The happiness we spoke of in *Ahavas Hashem* comes from the confidence of knowing that since Hashem created the system for us, we can succeed. The happiness that comes from *Yiras Hashem* comes from taking control of our actions and thoughts, and becoming great.

MITZVAH REVIEW

Constant **5** מצוה
Mitzvah תמידית

יְרְאַת ה' —
FEARING HASHEM

W e defined *Yiras Hashem* as an awareness that reward
and punishment are not arbitrary — they are natural,
real consequences of mitzvos and sins. Mitzvos earn us a
measure of the ultimate pleasure of basking in Hashem's
Presence — which, we have seen, is the entire purpose of
Creation — and sins create blemishes on our soul that prevent
us from appreciating that pleasure. Hashem will not allow
sins to go unpunished, unless we eradicate them through
repentance, because if He were to overlook them, our soul
could never attain the perfection necessary for enjoying the
ultimate pleasure.

Yiras Hashem does not contradict *Ahavas Hashem*; rather, the
two are complementary. When we realize that Hashem loves
us so much that He will not allow us to suffice with the temporal, empty pleasures of this world, but will ensure that we
receive the ultimate reward, our love for Him becomes more
meaningful and intense.

We fear Hashem only because we are aware of the consequences of acting in a way that is ruinous to our quest for
perfection. Therefore, in order to build *Yiras Hashem*, we must
take stock of our actions through regularly scheduled *cheshbon*

hanefesh (introspective evaluation of our conduct) to ascertain whether we are on the correct path to perfection. Since Hashem's measurement of reward and punishment is extremely precise, even taking into account the secondary and tertiary motives for our actions, we must learn to be honest with ourselves and be aware of the motives that are driving our behavior.

Practical Applications of Yiras Hashem

(1) Rambam discusses a form of *Yiras Hashem* that defines the word *yirah* as "awe." We develop awe by studying Hashem's greatness (as we did to build *Ahavah*) and realizing how overwhelmingly insignificant we are in comparison to Him.

(2) Consider the spiritual consequences of your actions as seriously as you consider their physical consequences.

(3) Identify the sources of your fear. Try to eradicate fear of events or circumstances that will affect you in the physical world but have no effect on the true purpose of your existence. Instead, be fearful of the destruction that misdeeds will bring upon you for all eternity.

(4) Implement a system of *cheshbon hanefesh*, careful accounting of your deeds. The following is a summary of the steps in *cheshbon hanefesh*:

    a. Be certain that you have crystallized your worldview, and that you live only for the true purpose of the world — to attain *shleimus* (spiritual perfection). Don't just "live with" Torah and mitzvos — live *for* them.

b. Set specific goals toward attaining *shleimus* and track your progress regularly to assure that you are moving in that direction. At its highest level, this step of *cheshbon hanefesh* will have you acting only after you consider the implications an action will have on your quest for perfection. At the very least, you should periodically examine your past actions to determine whether they were in line with that quest.

c. When you find that you have acted in a way that will interfere with your advance toward perfection, examine the circumstances that led you to act that way and determine how to prevent yourself from repeating that error in the future.

d. Question your questioning: ascertain that your introspection is leading you toward growth, not toward paralysis.

(5) Be honest with yourself. Examine the motives — both primary and secondary — that fuel your actions.

(6) Erect safeguards to prevent yourself from acting in a way that runs counter to your understanding of the purpose of the world.

Additive Effect of Yiras Hashem

In *Ahavas Hashem,* we learned that love of Hashem means to love the God that we came to know and understand in the first three mitzvos. In *Yirah* we learn that that love cannot be shallow; it must be based on the awareness that Hashem will cause us to attain perfection one way or another — even if it means cleansing us of our sins through suffering.

In the practical realm, *Yiras Hashem* manifests itself as a constant awareness of God's Omnipresence, which prevents us from risking our spiritual success, no matter how significant the perceived benefit.

מִצְוָה תְּמִידִי
CONSTANT MITZVAH
6

שֶׁלֹּא לָתוּר אַחַר מַחֲשֶׁבֶת
הַלֵּב וּרְאִיַּת הָעֵינַיִם

Do Not Stray After Your Heart and Your Eyes

שֶׁלֹּא לָתוּר אַחַר מַחֲשֶׁבֶת הַלֵּב וּרְאִיַּת הָעֵינַיִם
Not to stray after the thoughts of the heart and the sight of the eyes

שֶׁלֹּא נָתוּר אַחַר מַחֲשֶׁבֶת הַלֵּב וּרְאִיַּת הָעֵינַיִם, שֶׁנֶּאֱמַר [במדבר טו, לט], "וְלֹא תָתוּרוּ אַחֲרֵי לְבַבְכֶם וְאַחֲרֵי עֵינֵיכֶם אֲשֶׁר אַתֶּם זֹנִים אַחֲרֵיהֶם". עִנְיַן לַאו זֶה שֶׁנִּמְנַעְנוּ שֶׁלֹּא נְיַחֵד מַחְשְׁבוֹתֵינוּ לַחְשׁוֹב בְּדֵעוֹת שֶׁהֵם הֵפֶךְ הַדַּעַת שֶׁהַתּוֹרָה בְּנוּיָה עָלָיו, לְפִי שֶׁאֶפְשָׁר לָבוֹא מִתּוֹךְ כָּךְ לְמִינוּת. אֶלָּא, אִם יַעֲלֶה עַל לִבּוֹ רוּחַ לַחְשׁוֹב בְּאוֹתָן דֵּעוֹת הָרָעִים, יְקַצֵּר מַחְשַׁבְתּוֹ בָּהֶם וְיִשְׁנֶה לַחְשׁוֹב בְּדַרְכֵי הַתּוֹרָה הָאֲמִתִּיִּים וְהַטּוֹבִים. וּכְמוֹ כֵן שֶׁלֹּא יִרְדּוֹף הָאָדָם אַחַר מַרְאֵה עֵינָיו. וּבִכְלַל זֶה שֶׁלֹּא לִרְדּוֹף אַחַר תַּאֲווֹת הָעוֹלָם הַזֶּה, כִּי אַחֲרִיתָם רָעָה וּכְדַי בִּזָּיוֹן וָקֶצֶף, וְזֶה שֶׁאָמְרוּ זִכְרוֹנָם לִבְרָכָה [ספרי כאן], "וְלֹא תָתוּרוּ אַחֲרֵי לְבַבְכֶם", זוֹ מִינוּת, "וְאַחֲרֵי עֵינֵיכֶם", זוֹ זְנוּת, שֶׁנֶּאֱמַר [שפטים יד, ג], "וַיֹּאמֶר שִׁמְשׁוֹן אֶל אָבִיו אוֹתָהּ קַח לִי כִּי הִיא יָשְׁרָה בְעֵינָי".

We are not to stray after the thoughts of our heart and the sight of our eyes, as stated in the verse, "Do not stray after your heart and after your eyes, after which you wander" (*Bamidbar* 15:39).

The purpose of this prohibition is to prevent us from focusing our thoughts on philosophies that run counter to the understanding upon which the Torah is built, because one can come to heresy by doing so. Rather, if such thoughts encroach on one's mind, he should cut his thoughts short and begin to think about the true and perfect ways of the Torah. Similarly, one should not pursue the sights perceived by his eyes. This prohibition also precludes us from pursuing the temptations of this world, for their end is bad, and they are worthy of shame and anger.

These ideas are expressed in the words of *Chazal* (*Sifri* to this verse): "Do not stray after your heart" refers to heresy, and "after your eyes" refers to lustful activities, as stated in the verse, "Shimshon said to his father, 'Take her for me, for she is fitting in my eyes'" (*Shoftim* 14:3).

(*Chinuch, Mitzvah* 387)

Constant Mitzvah
6
מצוה תמידית

שֶׁלֹּא לָתוּר אַחַר מַחֲשֶׁבֶת הַלֵּב וּרְאִיַּת הָעֵינַיִם — DO NOT STRAY AFTER YOUR HEART AND EYES

I: Avoiding Distraction

I n the last of the Six Constant Mitzvos, the Torah commands us: וְלֹא תָתוּרוּ אַחֲרֵי לְבַבְכֶם וְאַחֲרֵי עֵינֵיכֶם, *Do not stray after your heart and after your eyes (Bamidbar* 15:39). A superficial glance at this mitzvah leads us to believe that the Torah considers the eyes and the heart to be inherently evil. A Midrash (*Tanchuma, Parashas Shelach* 15, cited in *Rashi*) verifies this understanding, stating that the eyes and the heart are two agents that lead the body to sin: the eyes see, the heart covets, and the body follows through and commits the sin.

This label seems rather harsh. What is wrong with the heart? Are the emotions of the heart uniformly bad? And why are our eyes considered evil? The eyes provide us with perception, with curiosity — they open us up to the world. Why are they considered evil?

Furthermore, we find many instances in which the Torah speaks highly of the heart and eyes. Hashem says: תְּנָה בְנִי לִבְּךָ לִי, *My child, give your **heart** to Me* (*Mishlei* 23:26). We are commanded to serve Hashem with all our *heart* (*Devarim* 11:13). The Sanhedrin were called עֵינֵי הָעֵדָה, *the **eyes** of the assembly* (*Bamidbar* 15:24). King David was described as having *beautiful eyes* (*I Shmuel* 16:12) because he accepted the rulings of the Sanhedrin (*Bereishis Rabbah* 63:8). Apparently, the heart and eyes are not necessarily bad. So why does the Torah command us not to stray after them?

Furthermore, it is also difficult to understand what the Torah demands of us in this mitzvah. The emotions that our heart feels and the perception that our eyes provide seem to be an essential part of us. Is the Torah telling us not to stray after ourselves? Can we be expected to negate and nullify the feelings that automatically enter our heart, or the sights that enter our eyes?

The key to understanding this mitzvah lies in the answer to some more puzzling questions.

The Talmud (*Berachos* 12b) teaches that not straying after our heart means not to involve ourselves in heresy, and not straying after our eyes means not to involve ourselves in immoral acts. Logic would dictate that the first five constant mitzvos make this sixth one unnecessary.

The first mitzvah, *Emunah*, requires us to know that Hashem exists, and to make sure that our actions reflect that knowledge. The second mitzvah, *Lo Yihiyeh*, commands us not to seek success through means that are detached from God. The third mitzvah, *Yichud Hashem*, requires us to recognize that nothing truly exists aside from Hashem. The fourth mitzvah is *Ahavas Hashem*, to love Hashem. It is obvious that anyone who fulfills these four mitzvos cannot involve himself in heresy. The fifth mitzvah, *Yiras Hashem*, require us to realize that there are serious consequences to our actions. A person who has *Yiras Hashem* will not get involved in heretical *or* lustful activities.

Why do we need a separate commandment not to engage in

such activities if we are already prohibited from doing so by the first five mitzvos? Furthermore, according to the Talmud's interpretation of this mitzvah, why does the Torah tell us not to stray after our heart and mind — why doesn't it state clearly: "Do not be heretical and do not lust"?

◈§ Emotions and Perception: Objective or Subjective?

The first step to answering these questions lies in differentiating between *Lo Sasuru*, the commandment not to stray, and the five constant mitzvos that go before it. While the first five mitzvos are rooted in philosophy, with practical applications emerging by implication, *Lo Sasuru* is a practical mitzvah *only*. The first five mitzvos laid the groundwork for our spiritual success in this world. By the time we reach the mitzvah of *Lo Sasuru*, we already know that Hashem exists, that no other force contains any power, that Hashem is One, that we love Him, and that we fear Him. We know that success is measured in terms of spiritual perfection. We know that everything else is temporal and superficial. We know that if we indulge in short-lived pleasures, we will pay a heavy price.

We *know* all that, but then we are suddenly overcome by temptation. Someone or something enticing is before us and we *know* that we should avert our gaze. We are sitting at a computer, and we *know* that clicking the mouse-button will take us to a place where we don't belong. There is a juicy piece of gossip on the tip of our tongue, and we *know* that we should not say it. But there is still a struggle. And we tell ourselves, "I know this is wrong. I know it doesn't pay. I know this is spiritual suicide."

But we still feel torn. The battle rages on despite all the knowledge. We know what we should do, but … but … and then it is too late.

What happened? We knew that we were doing the wrong thing. Why did we lose the battle?

We lost the battle because we got distracted. We could not hold onto the values we have worked so hard to incorporate into our life, because we got sidetracked.

Lo Sasuru does not require us to learn anything new. It requires us not to get distracted. It requires us to remain focused on what we already know, and not to let our hearts and eyes lead us into territory that contradicts our *weltanschauung*.

Let us look at the roles that the heart and eyes play in our life, and see why the Torah singles them out as the organs that we must be careful not to stray after.

• The Heart

In a physical sense, the heart supplies energy to the body by pumping blood to the systems and supplying them with life-sustaining oxygen. In a spiritual sense, too, the heart is the organ that represents human emotion, the most powerful force in the world. A person who feels strongly about something will pursue it relentlessly, whereas a person who is ambivalent will not. In terms of decision making, therefore, the heart, as the seat of emotion, is crucial.

But are emotions always rational? Can we control them? Take a look at people reading a novel. When they sit down on the sofa and begin to read, they know that they are about to enter the world of imagination. They know that it is fiction. Before long, however, the reader begins to feel an emotional attachment to the characters. A moving novel will cause a reader to live through the trials and tribulations together with the characters. Try to stop someone in the middle of a novel and point out that the fear he is feeling for the hero or heroine in danger is all for naught, because he or she never existed. Will it make a difference? Hardly. Their emotions have taken control of them.

The same happens when people watch a play. They know quite well that they are about to enter a fantasy world. But as the scenes unfold before their eyes, they begin to cry for the characters. Why are they crying? Tell a person weeping at a play that the characters are not really in trouble — the actors simply make it seem that they are. The tears will still fall. Once emotion stirs, it is incontrollable.

Since the heart responds so readily to trivial or false signals, can we trust it to make our decisions in life? Much as the heart is crucial, we must remember that it is no more than a muscle. Like the heart of every other member of the animal kingdom, the human heart instinctively produces emotions that protect us or help us survive. But as humans, we must strive for more. We must place our heart in the service of our superior intellect.

• The Eyes

The eyes are equally unreliable.

Psychologists often use pictures to diagnose problems in children. They show sets of pictures depicting people in ordinary situations, and they ask children to describe what they see. One child will look at a picture of a boy standing next to his mother and say, "I see a happy boy." Another child will look at the very same picture and see a sad boy.

Assuming that the facial expressions of the boy in the picture are equivocal, is either child wrong in his or her assessment? No. One child has a set belief that a child in his mother's company is happy; the other is transferring his own ill feelings toward his mother onto the child in the picture. The way we see things is not objective. We often see what we expect and want to see.

Since our emotions often control us, rather than being controlled by us, we cannot rely on them to direct our lives, and we cannot rely on our eyes to provide insight into the world.

Let's examine a practical application of this concept.

Although addictions will usually develop into a chemical dependency, they do not start that way. And they do not begin with logic, either. No one will tell you that he believes ideologically that he should be drinking, gambling, or smoking cigarettes. If you catch an alcoholic in a sober moment and ask him why he was created, he is unlikely to reply, "I was created to drink myself into a stupor and roll around in the gutter." Alcoholism, and many other addictions, begin with a need for a lift from downtrodden emotions. A person who is depressed will seek some sort of temporary relief, and try something that he knows quite well may hurt him. Why? Because emotions overpower logic.

Emotions will also prevent an addict from improving. While sober, an alcoholic can think about his job, his family, and his goals. He can decide that he should never have started drinking, and that getting drunk leads to trouble. He can use such a moment to seek help. Why doesn't he? Because he is emotionally connected to the freedom from reality that his addiction affords.

An alcoholic's view of the world can also become distorted. The story is told of an alcoholic whose family could not convince him to seek help. One day, his son saw a fellow rolling in the streets with a bottle of whiskey in his hand, singing loudly, blocking traffic, and making a fool of himself. He figured that this was his chance to make his father aware of the effects of alcohol. He ran home, and to his relief, his father was sober. He grabbed his father's hand and took him to see the drunk. "Father, do you see how destructive alcohol is?"

The father shook his hand free from his son's, walked purposefully toward the drunk, and said, "Sir, where did you get such good whiskey?"

The son saw a fellow who was allowing alcohol to destroy his life; the father saw a man who succeeded in finding a substance he enjoyed so much. Two hearts, two sets of emotions. Two sets of eyes, two perceptions.

Thankfully, most of us are not tempted to drink or engage in similarly harmful activity. That does not mean, however, that we are safe from the dangers of overpowering emotions and distorted perception.

When a person gives in to a strong temptation to sin, is he denying that Hashem exists? Does he want to dispense with his love and fear of Hashem? Certainly not. He simply loses control. His emotions overpower him.

Once we have mastered the first five constant mitzvos, the Torah does not need to command us not to engage in heresy or lust, because we will not be heretical or lustful — at least not intentionally. The first five mitzvos do not guarantee, however, that we will refrain from sinning. Why? Because our emotions and perceptions will take control of us from time to time, and all the logic of *Emunah, Lo Yihiyeh,* and the other mitzvos will go out the window.

Now we come to a crucial question. If emotions and perception are so powerful, if they can hijack our thoughts and cause us to do things that we know are wrong, what alternative do we have?

The answer lies in the wording of this commandment: don't stray *after* your heart and eyes.

We can compare our heart and eyes to a seeing-eye dog. If a blind person allows an untrained dog to lead him around, the dog may lead him into trees, busy streets, and other dangerous areas. If the dog is trained properly, however, it can guide its master into safe territory and protect him from danger.

The first five constant mitzvos teach us to appreciate spirituality, to yearn for the eternal rather than the temporary. But the world is full of distractions. There are so many opportunities for instant gratification. If we do not take charge, our heart and eyes will, necessarily, find replacements for our true inner yearnings. The yearning for eternity will be replaced with a sense of ego. The yearning for eternal pleasure will be replaced with a desire for instant gratification.

Lo Sasuru requires us to stay one step ahead of our heart and eyes, and cause them to feel emotion and to perceive in accordance with the truths that we have internalized in the previous five mitzvos. We must use them to protect the *Emunah, Yichud, Ahavah,* and *Yirah* that we have already developed in the previous mitzvos. We can program our heart and eyes to energize us for spiritual growth, but if we leave them on their own, they will focus only on the mundane and superficial pleasures of this world.

⊷§ *Acharei Levavchem*: "I Feel Like ..."

Until now, we have been discussing the heart and eyes as one unit. We have defined the mitzvah of *Lo Sasuru* as the need to control our emotions and perception rather than have them control us. Before we can learn how to take control of our heart and eyes, we must first learn to differentiate between them.

The heart and eyes both seem to send us the same message. The heart represents *feelings*: "I feel like doing ..." The eyes send signals to the mind that are interpreted as, "I want ..." These are both instinctive reflexes to external stimuli, but they are a bit different. The emotions represented by the heart may or may not be accompanied by an incontrollable drive to follow through on them. They may not cause us to sin irresponsibly. Rather, they affect our decision-making process and cause us to make improper choices.

Let us look at an example.

A person who has chosen between a professional career and a more spiritually-oriented occupation will often be affected by an emotion. The choice between a life devoted to the thankless task of helping the Jewish people and one of relative comfort provided by a "real job" is a difficult one. The first five constant mitzvos are necessary in making the initial decision. Clarity in the purpose of the world will certainly move a person in a certain direction. But *Lo Sasuru* will be vital in the aftermath. Someone who has made a philosophical decision to use his talents in the most meaningful manner possible may later find himself plagued by feelings of disappointment from time to time. "I could have been a millionaire," he may feel, "and instead I am struggling to make a living." Or "I could have been a famous doctor, and instead I am hated as the walking, interfering conscience of the neighborhood."

Realize that in this case, the heart does not develop a *craving* to make money. That might be the problem that a gambler or workaholic faces. The problem here is the involuntary feeling of disillusionment that begins to develop in the heart, saying, "You must change your direction in life." Allowing that feeling to flower and bloom is straying after the heart. It is particularly difficult to deal with such a feeling, because, as opposed to a lustful drive, it is hard to recognize the wickedness of the heart and label it as such.

Let us look at another example of an emotion that is unaccompanied by drive, but is harmful nonetheless.

> *A Holocaust survivor recalled that he once saw a group of defeated, tired SS men being held by the Russian army. He said that he and his fellow survivors felt bad for their former oppressors for a few minutes.*

When we hear this story, we understand the emotion felt by this survivor. With the existing mindset in the world nowadays set by Western liberals, we consider compassion to be the closest thing to perfection. And a Jewish heart is naturally compassionate. But *Chazal* (*Tanchuma, Metzora* 1) warn us not to fall into this trap, because "One who is merciful toward the cruel will end up being cruel toward the merciful." They derived this lesson from a painful episode in our history.

Hashem sent the prophet Shmuel to King Shaul to command him to wipe out all of Amalek. Shaul did not have the heart to kill everyone. He left the women, animals, and Agag, the king of Amalek, alive. Hashem sent Shmuel to inform Shaul that he would lose the kingdom because of his failure to carry out Hashem's decree.

Compassion is failure? Yes. Like any other emotion, compassion must be directed. If it is the product of a misguided heart, it must be eradicated. In Shaul's case, it was misplaced compassion. The Midrash points out that not very much later, the very same Shaul ordered that the pious Kohanim of Nov should be killed, because he was under the impression that they were sheltering David, who had been anointed as his successor.

Chazal determined that Shaul's problem was that he followed his heart. When his heart told him to be compassionate toward the Amalekites, he followed it. And when his heart later told him to protect his kingdom and his family's future, he followed it in an act that totally lacked compassion.

When a Holocaust survivor says that he felt bad for imprisoned Nazi torturers and murderers, he is demonstrating his Jewish heart. The Torah warns us not to follow our heart in such cases. Our values become distorted when we accept emotions that should not exist. We must learn to control and redirect them when they are inappropriate.

We are required — *required* — to develop a passionate hatred toward Amalek. This mitzvah is unusual; the Torah does not command us to foment hatred in any other case. But this mitzvah also represents a basic belief of Judaism. The heart is not sensible. It creates inexplicable feelings, and we are in danger of acting on those feelings. The heart must be guided. In the unusual case of Amalek, we must enlist its services to bring us to adequate hatred toward them so that we can fulfill the commandment to eradicate them. Regarding other mitzvos, we must learn to program the heart in such a way that it will provide us with the energy needed to carry them out. And above all, when we feel our heart developing a program of its own, independent of Hashem's will, we must learn to ignore it.

◆§ Acharei Eineichem: "I Want"

We find a slight difference in the language King David used when praying for success in controlling various aspects of the body. He said: הַט לִבִּי אֶל עֵדְוֹתֶיךָ וְאַל אֶל בָּצַע, *Incline my heart toward Your testimonies and not to greed* (119:36), followed by: הַעֲבֵר

עֵינַי מֵרְאוֹת שָׁוְא‎, *Avert my eyes from seeing futility* (ibid. v. 37).

At the very beginning of the Code of Law, *Tur* explains the difference. We are not forced to process external stimuli that affect our heart. We can choose to ignore them and incline our heart toward good even after it senses something evil. We do not have the same opportunity when it comes to our eyes. As soon as something improper passes before us, our brain processes the information and the image weakens our value system. The eyes, therefore, must be *prevented* from seeing these images, for even the slightest glance at evil can lead us astray. And the image remains in our subconscious and can be reawakened at any time.

When the Torah commands us not to stray after our eyes, then, it is not referring to a feeling, but to a craving or a drive. The eyes provide us with impulses that say, "I *must* do this. Now."

An alcoholic, for instance, is not following his heart. He may be crying deep down. He is following his eyes. When a craving takes hold of him, his better judgment goes out the window. An impulse shopper follows his eyes, not his heart. It is automatic and spontaneous. No thought, no emotion: "I want it."

ᴥ§ Don't Stray: A Practical Guide

DAY 48

Now that we have defined the roles that the heart and eyes play, we can learn how to counter the individual threats they present.

Drunk driving is considered a serious crime, and rightfully so. But a drunk might argue that there should be no penalty for drunk driving. The more drunk a person is, the less control he has over his abilities. Why do we fault a person whose thinking was impaired by alcohol for choosing to drive and put others in danger?

The answer is that we expect people to make responsible decisions *before* they begin to drink so that they will not drive under the influence. We expect them to deposit their car keys with someone who is not planning to drink.

Similarly, since emotions and perceptions are so overwhelming, we are most likely to succeed in *Lo Sasuru* by following the saying, "An ounce of prevention is worth a pound of cure."

The primary goal in combating the natural feelings produced by our heart is to avoid them by developing more powerful ones for the truths that we have come to know in the first five constant mitzvos.

Let's take laziness as an example. When we get into a rut of laziness, we feel as though we are physically unable to move. It seems to paralyze us in a *physical* sense. But laziness is an emotion. We all know people who seem to have a desperate need to accomplish more and more. Such people rarely fall into the trap of laziness, because their emotional need to move forward is more powerful than that of laziness. It is the people whose dreams are always centered around their next vacation and early retirement who constantly find themselves sitting on the couch trying to get up some energy to move, because they have no emotions to counter their laziness.

What is the solution? Hashem says: תְּנָה בְנִי לִבְּךָ לִי, *My child, give your heart to Me* (*Mishlei* 23:26).

Take your heart, and submit it to your intellect. Emotions can be combatted only with more intense emotions, which, in turn, can be created only by the mind. As we develop clarity in our understanding of these mitzvos, we should become "emotionally involved" with them. We should walk around feeling, "*Ashreinu, mah tov chelkeinu,*" feeling fortunate that we have the opportunity to take part in the purpose of this world, and that we will eventually experience the most pleasurable reward possible in the World to Come. The clearer we are in our purpose, the more emotion we will generate for it. These emotions can become so strong that they will make us unyielding to the threat of the heart's challenging emotions.

The approach to not straying after the eyes is extremely different. The bad news is that there is no way to enlist the eyes into the service of the intellect. Our only option is to fight the desires and cravings that the eyes perceive. How?

We learn from King David that the first step in preventing sin is to avoid situations in which we may be tempted to indulge in cravings or senseless passion. We must face the difficult reality that we are human, and that we have a *yetzer hara* inside us that tries constantly to lead us toward sin. Yes, we realize that he is part of the great purpose of the world (see pages 133-135), but we must still admit to ourselves that we are often too weak to resist his constant badgering. If we are honest about how much of a presence he is in our system, we will train ourselves to run away from potential temptation.

> *A talmid asked his mashgiach, Rabbi Eliyahu Lopian, for permission to travel to a cousin's wedding in a different city. When the mashgiach heard which city it was, he did not want to grant permission. "That city is known for the improper mode of dress of its residents," he explained. "It is not the place for a ben Torah."*
>
> *"But Rebbi," the boy protested, "I work hard on guarding my eyes and thoughts, and I am not affected by this problem."*
>
> *Rav Elyah drew out a generous sum of money from his pocket and handed it to the boy. "I am nearly 90 years old and I am blind in one eye," he said, "and I still feel the yetzer hara stirring inside of me. If you can go to that city without being affected, you had better take this money and see a doctor."*

The good news is that cravings are not in sole possession of the *yetzer hara*. We can develop cravings for spirituality as well. The same King David who begged Hashem to avert his eyes from evil lest he be led astray also said: *I*, חִשַּׁבְתִּי דְרָכָי וָאָשִׁיבָה רַגְלַי אֶל עֵדֹתֶיךָ

planned my path, and returned my feet to Your testimonies (*Tehillim* 119:59). A Midrash (*Vayikra Rabbah* 35:1) explains that King David would walk out of his palace each day with a schedule for the day, but his feet would involuntarily carry him to the study hall to study Torah. He had developed a reflex that made Torah study his default position.

Apparently, aside from controlling our eyes and avoiding situations filled with temptation, we can also develop new cravings and habits. We must become experts at making the correct choices so that it becomes second nature. Our feet, hands, and all the mechanical organs should be trained to serve Hashem automatically.

Certainly, we must be aware of the potential pitfall of beginning to run on "automatic pilot" and losing all the feeling in our service of Hashem, but it is much easier to fight the problem of following good habits out of rote than it is to fight bad habits.

II: Maintaining Success

The most challenging aspect of the mitzvah not to stray after our heart and eyes is that we were each equipped with only one set of these vital organs. Our entire understanding of the world is based on the perceptions and emotions provided by our eyes and heart. It seems that they are the only organs we have that we can use to monitor our actions and emotions. But how can we rely on such unreliable organs to police themselves? How do we know whether they are providing us with true perspectives of ourselves, or whether they are fooling us into believing that we are in control, when in truth we are following them?

Some people facing this challenge will say, "There is no way to figure out the truth," and simply hope for the best. On a certain level, it is true; there *is* no way to be absolutely sure that we are on the correct path. But to surrender is not an option. We know that we are here for a purpose, and that there must be some way to fulfill our mission in life. There must be some way for our heart and eyes to police themselves.

⊷§ Empowering the Intellect

Mesillas Yesharim (Chapters 2 and 3) is extremely bothered by this problem. In response, he notes that *Chazal's* comparison of our journey through this world to a person walking in the darkness of night is particularly fitting. There are two dangers one faces when walking in the dark. One is danger of the unseen. A person traveling in the dark can fall into an unseen pit. Similarly, a person can spend his years on earth in petty pursuit of meaningless goals simply because he is unaware of any higher calling. He never knew that there was more meaning to life. The other danger is of mistaken identification of dimly lit objects. A person walking in darkness might walk into a pillar because he thinks that it is a person who will step aside when he approaches. Similarly, a person traveling through this world might spend his time chasing some sort of goal that he mistakenly identifies as good, when in truth it is evil. What alternative do we have?

Mesillas Yesharim writes that we can succeed only if we take advice from those who have already met with success: *Chazal* (*Bava Basra* 78b), whose advice was, "*Bo'u cheshbon* — come make a *cheshbon* of your actions."

We have already discussed the need for *cheshbon hanefesh* in detail in the context of *Yiras Hashem* (see pages 206-214), but *Lo Sasuru* requires a more basic form of *cheshbon hanefesh*.

> *A fine Jew named Mel managed to escape Europe and made it to the United States penniless. A kindhearted fellow offered to teach him how to bake, and Mel became an excellent baker. He was not much of a businessman, however, so when it came time to go out on his own, he took a partner who would handle the business end. The partner told him that they should begin by offering their pastries at a reduced price so that they would draw customers, and Mel went along with the plan.*
>
> *Mel's cakes were so good that before long he became one of the most popular sources for kosher pastries in the New York area. His partner spent his time courting more and more customers, and they enjoyed great success. They were so popular that they were being honored by organizations for their services.*
>
> *One day they ran into some trouble calculating their revenues, and they hired an accountant to review their books. The accountant sat with their ledgers for some time, and then leveled them with disheartening news: they were bankrupt.*
>
> *Their initial reaction was to blame … the accountant. "How can we be bankrupt?" they protested. "We own the most popular bakery in the area!"*

It took a while for them to figure out where they had gone wrong. In their excitement over their popularity, they had forgotten to raise their prices. They were still offering their pastries at the same bargain prices as when they started. At each event they catered they lost money.

When we discussed *cheshbon hanefesh* in *Yiras Hashem*, we were referring to the need to keep track of our life goals and our deeds. *Lo Sasuru* requires a much more basic form of *cheshbon*: guaranteeing that we are not getting distracted and that we remember why we are "in business." Are we still striving to fulfill the goals we set for ourselves in *Emunah*, *Lo Yihiyeh*, *Yichud*, *Ahavah* and *Yiras Hashem*, or are we following our emotions and cravings into nothingness? Are we making progress, or are we like Mel the baker, so blinded by "success" that we don't realize we are running ourselves bankrupt?

It is difficult to evaluate our own progress. But *Mesillas Yesharim* teaches us that it can be done. Our intellect is ultimately the most powerful force in our system — if we invest effort into empowering it over our emotions. If we try to use raw emotion to monitor emotion or raw perception to monitor perception, we will fail. But if the heart and eyes are connected to the intellect, they can police themselves.

We must — *must* — take the time every now and then to reexamine what it is that we are living for. In the first five mitzvos we have learned that there is a purpose to this world, that we play an important role in that purpose, that every event in our lives is connected to our role, and that we can love the challenge that the purpose presents. *Lo Sasuru* is there to protect the other five mitzvos, to ensure that we are still living for that purpose.

Cheshbon hanefesh is the only way to guarantee that we remain focused on a life full of meaning, so that we can enjoy the ultimate pleasure of basking in the Glory of Hashem's *Shechinah* when the world reaches perfection.

MITZVAH REVIEW

Constant Mitzvah 6 מצוה תמידית

שֶׁלֹּא לָתוּר אַחַר מַחֲשֶׁבֶת הַלֵּב וּרְאִיַּת הָעֵינַיִם — DO NOT STRAY AFTER YOUR HEART AND EYES

L o *Sasuru* is a mitzvah that protects the five that precede it. It is the means of assuring our success in implementing the other constant mitzvos and preventing us from becoming blinded by emotions and cravings that run counter to the outlook on life that we have developed through the study of the constant mitzvos.

The heart, which represents the seat of emotion, often sends us messages that contradict reality. In the spiritual realm, those messages might manifest themselves as feelings of regret for our choices to devote ourselves to Torah and mitzvos. Those feelings might not be accompanied by an overwhelming drive to act incorrectly, but they will nevertheless cast a pall over our service of Hashem.

The eyes perceive sights that can lead to cravings, which can overwhelm us and distract us from the truths that we have come to know, just long enough to cause us to sin.

Since emotions and cravings are hard to quell once they begin to fester, the key to success is prevention. Thus, the mitzvah is phrased as "Don't stray *after* your heart and eyes." Rather than straying *after* your heart and eyes, put these essential organs to use in the service of Hashem so that they are not free to wander. Instead of allowing yourself to become subservient to them, let them serve you.

Practical Applications of Lo Sasuru

(1) Develop a strong emotional bond with Torah, mitzvos, and service of Hashem, which will fill your heart with emotions that promote your quest for perfection, and thereby prevent you from developing contradictory emotions.

(2) Avoid situations in which your eyes might see something that could lead you to sin, because a craving can develop from the slightest perception. We can also develop cravings for spirituality, which manifest themselves as learning to choose correctly as a matter of routine (but not out of rote).

(3) As a completion of the *cheshbon hanefesh* process that you started in *Yiras Hashem*, set aside time occasionally to review all of the insights that you have gained during your study of the Six Constant Mitzvos. This will ensure that you have not become distracted, and that your actions still reflect those mitzvos and the purpose they represent.

Additive Effect of Lo Sasuru

The first five mitzvos require us to have specific thought processes or feelings reflected in our actions:

- *Emunah* requires us to ensure that our actions reflect our *knowledge* of Hashem's existence, and His purpose in creating the universe — namely, for us to perfect ourselves so we can enjoy the reward we earned in the World to Come.

- *Lo Yihiyeh* adds an awareness that no other forces have power to influence us, and a requirement to live our lives *only* for the purpose of Creation.

- *Yichud Hashem* teaches us that all that exists is Hashem, and that *all* forces and circumstances in the world are there to bring us closer to perfection.

- *Ahavas Hashem* requires us to feel love for Hashem, and to enjoy participating in the quest for perfection.

- *Yiras Hashem* is a mitzvah to fear the possibility of ruining our lives by ignoring the true purpose of Creation.

Lo Sasuru protects those mitzvos. It requires us to take steps to avoid getting distracted and losing sight of our true goals and mission.

עשה מצות תמידיות

Epilogue

Epilogue

In our discussion of the Six Constant Mitzvos, we have attempted to show how the six mitzvos are interconnected and dependent upon one another. In many instances, however, we had to sacrifice the forest for the trees — i.e., we could not focus on common threads that run through the mitzvos, lest we complicate the individual principles set forth by each mitzvah. Now that we have completed our study, however, it would be informative to study the beauty and unity inherent in the Six Constant Mitzvos.

We defined each of the first five mitzvos on two tracks. In the first one, which we will call the "Understanding and Relationship" track, we developed a deep understanding of Hashem and explained how a Jew is supposed to relate to Him. In the second one, which we will call the "Purpose" track, we focused on Hashem's purpose for this world, and we discussed how we should take part in, and relate to, that purpose.

≈§ Understanding and Relationship Track

(1) **Emunah**: We defined *Emunah* as clear-cut *knowledge* just of Hashem's existence. We explained that as opposed to just "faith" or "belief," a deep-seated knowledge of His existence will prevent a person from acting in a way that counters that knowledge.

(2) **Lo Yihiyeh** forbids us to believe that any force other than Hashem possesses power, even if we realize that it is a mere servant to Him.

(3) **Yichud Hashem** requires us to recognize that Hashem is One, which means that nothing other than God has true existence.

(4) **Ahavas Hashem** is the commandment to love Hashem, which can be achieved through study of His Torah and creations, and by sacrificing for His sake.

(5) **Yiras Hashem:** In terms of understanding and relating to Hashem, *Yiras Hashem* means to be in *awe* of Him.[1] We develop this awe when we realize our overwhelming insignificance in comparison with Him.

◄§ Purpose Track

(1) **Emunah** requires us to realize that Hashem must have created this world for a purpose. That purpose is to benefit mortals by offering us the greatest pleasure possible: basking in His glory in the World to Come. Since we can experience that pleasure only if we earn it,[2] our role in this world is to pursue spiritual growth and perfect ourselves.[3]

---

1. Many commentators note that there are two forms of *Yiras Hashem*: *yiras haromemus* (fear of His Glory), which we would define as *awe*, and *yiras ha'onesh* (fear of punishment). We suggest that these two forms of *yirah* coexist in the two tracks we are presenting. *Yiras haromemus* is the awe that emanates from an awareness of the Greatness of Hashem and affects our understanding and relationship with Him (see *Rambam, Hilchos Yesodei HaTorah* 2:2), and *yiras ha'onesh* is the fear that we will not take part in His purpose for Creation, which, we will show, is part of the "purpose" track.

2. As explained in depth in *Yichud Hashem* (pages 133-135).

3. There are two reasons why we must perfect ourselves in order to receive reward in the World to Come. The first is because we cannot enjoy a reward that we did not earn, and the second is because the pleasure of the World to Come is not physical pleasure, but spiritual pleasure that cannot be appreciated by an imperfect soul. By way of analogy, a sunset can be described to a blind person, but only a seeing person can truly appreciate the beauty of a sunset. On an infinitely greater level, only souls that have attained *shleimus* (spiritual perfection) will enjoy the closeness to Hashem that we will experience in the World to Come.

(2) **Lo Yihiyeh** forbids us to live for any purpose other than the one for which Hashem created the world, because such an existence would be meaningless and hollow.

(3) **Yichud Hashem** teaches that because Hashem created this world *only* for the purpose of allowing us to grow and attain perfection, all events and circumstances we experience are orchestrated by Him in a way that aids our spiritual growth. Therefore, even the most ordinary aspects of life, and even those events and circumstances that seem to get in the way of our growth, must actually contain some opportunity for growth. The *yetzer hara* is part of this purpose, playing the role of a coach who continually challenges us in order to help us grow and attain perfection.

(4) **Ahavas Hashem** requires us to love Hashem in order to create a world of purposeful challenge for *our* sake, and for granting us the tools to overcome the challenges we face. A true *oheiv Hashem* loves life and appreciates each moment that he can spend perfecting himself.

(5) **Yiras Hashem** requires us to deepen our recognition that we are living not for this insignificant, fleeting world, but for the World to Come, where we will enjoy eternal reward. Therefore, we should not fear circumstances that will affect us only in this world; rather, we should be fearful of the possibility that our own actions may render us unable to attain the perfection necessary to enjoy the eternal reward.

L O SASURU IS UNIQUE in that it is not split into two tracks. It is a mitzvah not to get distracted and forget all of the awarenesses that we developed in the previous mitzvos — both in understanding and relating to Hashem, and in our need to take part in His purpose for the world.

The above two tracks are not mutually exclusive, nor can one be developed at the expense of the other. The "understanding and relationship" track provides the basic philosophy behind the "purpose" track. Successful implementation of these mitzvos is dependent upon studying and internalizing both tracks simultaneously.

◄§ Seeking Refuge in a Dangerous World

*C*hinuch finds a scriptural reference to the Six Constant Mitzvos in the verse: שֵׁשׁ עָרֵי מִקְלָט תִּהְיֶינָה לָכֶם, *there shall be six cities of refuge for you* (*Bamidbar* 35:13). *Pri Megadim* (Introduction to *Mishbetzos Zahav, Orach Chaim*) explains this comparison. A person who murders unintentionally is protected from an avenger of his victim's death as long as he stays within the boundaries of a city of refuge, but if he leaves the city he is no longer protected. So too, one who remains within the boundaries of these six mitzvos is *constantly* protected from all influences that seek to lead us away from Hashem and His Torah.

In modern times, this protection is more necessary than ever. When two nations are at war, and they sense that a conclusion is imminent, each side will use all forces and means at its disposal to deal the final deathblow to its opponent. So too, writes Rav Tzadok HaKohen of Lublin, when we are in the final throes of war with the *yetzer hara*, he will use all of the means at his disposal to deal us a deathblow. We must find the means to battle him successfully, lest we lose the battle.

In all likelihood, we are now witnessing the *yetzer hara*'s release of all forces at his disposal. A conclusion seems imminent. Levels of impurity that would have been extremely difficult to access in previous generations are now thrust upon us on billboards, at supermarket checkout counters, and in corner stores. Furthermore, technological advancement turns devices that we consider necessities for normative living, such as computers and cellular phones, into minefields for the soul. Because most of us are unable to live without the convenience afforded by modern life, it is difficult — almost impossible — for us to take *physical* refuge from these hazards.

Our hopes for success are therefore dependent upon building *spiritual* cities of refuge around ourselves. *Chinuch* and *Pri Megadim* teach that the Six Constant Mitzvos are those cities of refuge.

We cannot rely on them for refuge, however, if we simply study them once. We must review them and develop deeper understanding and awareness of them, until they are reflected in our every action.

The Six Constant Mitzvos can, and should, transform us and make us resistant to the dangers of the world around us, by causing us to seek nothing other than spiritual perfection and closeness to Hashem. In the merit of our study and implementation of these mitzvos, may we be delivered from those dangers, and may we earn the ultimate reward of basking in His Glory for all eternity.

This volume is part of
THE ARTSCROLL® SERIES
an ongoing project of
translations, commentaries and expositions on
Scripture, Mishnah, Talmud, Midrash, Halachah,
liturgy, history, the classic Rabbinic writings,
biographies and thought.

For a brochure of current publications
visit your local Hebrew bookseller
or contact the publisher:

Mesorah Publications, ltd

313 Regina Avenue
Rahway, New Jersey 07065
(718) 921-9000
www.artscroll.com